HERE AMONG STRANGERS

HERE
AMONG
STRANGERS

stories by

Serena Crawford

LOST HORSE PRESS

ACKNOWLEDGMENTS

I am grateful to the National Endowment for the Arts, Literary Arts, and the University of Oregon Creative Writing Program for their generous support.

My deepest thanks to those who have read my stories in various forms over the years, especially Peter Ho Davies, Chang-rae Lee, Paige Newman, and my peers in the University of Oregon Creative Writing Program. Thank you to Jess Bryant, Polly Buckingham, and the hard-working staff of Willow Springs Books. I am grateful to Lysley Tenorio for his encouragement and insight. This book would not be what it is without the eagle eye of David Wilkins.

These stories were published, sometimes in different form, in the following publications:

Another Chicago Magazine: "Here Among Strangers" as "Kippy's Return"
Ascent: "Silence"
Beloit Fiction Journal: "Ocean"
Epoch: "Mr. Lee"
The Florida Review: "My Brother's House"
The McNeese Review: "Chinatown"

FIRST EDITION

Cover Art: *The Protector* by Justin Duffus. 24"x12," oil on mylar, 2014. This and other works by Justin Duffus can be found at justinduffus.com.

Author Photo: T.S. Whalen

Cover Design: Kyle Thiele

Interior Design: Jess L. Bryant

LIBRARY OF CONGRESS CATALOGING-IN-PUBLICATION

Names: Crawford, Serena, author.
Title: Here among strangers / written by Serena Crawford.
Description: First edition. | Sandpoint, Idaho : Lost Horse Press, [2016]Identifiers: LCCN 2016002983 | ISBN 9780996858410 (softcover : acid-free paper)
Classification: LCC PS3603.R3973 A6 2016 | DDC 813/.6—dc23
LC record available at http://lccn.loc.gov/2016002983

CONTENTS

For David

CHINATOWN

My mother is waiting for me in short-term parking, winded, leaning against the passenger door of her car. She's holding a clipboard with a list of places she wants to go: first Costco, then Dollar Tree, then Walmart, then the Hostess Bakery Outlet, in that exact order. Ten years ago, she traveled the globe giving lectures on macroeconomic policy and strategic leadership; now this. Never mind that Dollar Tree is on the way to her favorite Costco, and Walmart on the opposite side of town, so that we will zigzag back and forth, wasting time and guzzling gas, or that she will tire after an hour because she is obese and takes an inordinate amount of medications for conditions she will not divulge. She has the list of items (Rolaids, batteries, Aleve), the prices she wants to compare. She has the coupons. My job is to drive, so she can examine the expiration dates and do her calculations.

We are not the greeting type—never have been—so I get down to business, pushing aside newspapers and brochures to make room in the trunk. I have a backpack and a suitcase—I only own what I can carry—which would immediately alert my sisters to the fact that I'm moving, but this is mere hand luggage to my mother.

"You look good," she says, which is weird, because we don't talk about these things. Besides, I don't. I have the vitamin-deficient pallor of someone who's lost a lot of blood.

I can't say the same for her. She's getting bigger by the minute. "The car's looking better," I remark.

The backseat is piled high with newspapers, but it's been worse. There was a time you couldn't see to back up, and another time a small sofa was strapped (for a year) to its roof. Two nights ago, my sisters had me on the phone, begging me to fly up to Portland, saying things had gotten bad again and Mom wouldn't let them inside her house. They'd already bought my ticket. "Gina, you're the only one she'll listen to," they said.

Both of them are prone to overreacting.

I could stay with one of them—they live only half an hour away—and walk back and forth between their shared duplex, hearing all about their kids' bedtime routines or home remedies for common warts, but neither of them understands the concept of personal space. Plus it makes them nervous if—God forbid—I eat with chopsticks.

My mother climbs into the passenger seat, winded again, and starts computing numbers on her clipboard, determining if the buy-one-get-one-free deal at Costco beats the printable coupon from Walmart.com. I get in behind the wheel.

"All set, Doctor?" I'm not mocking her; this is a term of endearment. Back when we were little, and she was getting her Ph.D., this is how my father addressed her whenever she came in the door.

"You don't need to go to the house, do you?" She looks up from her clipboard, her mouth crooked from the strain of my company and the excess flesh around her jowls. The house—a three-story Victorian with a dumbwaiter and a cupola—is where I grew up.

I'm thinking the wrong answer might send her into cardiac arrest, considering her health.

The water has been off in my building and I haven't showered for two days, but I tell her it can wait.

What my sisters don't understand is if you try to stop her, it only makes things worse. Let her do her thing, and she wears herself out.

First stop: Costco, land of the oversized. My mother fits right in. When we get to the entrance, a whoosh of air sucks us through. I have to jog to keep up with it. My mother barrels ahead, carried by the current, the nose of her cart perilously close to a display of LED flashlights. A man wearing old-fashioned hearing aids cuts me off, running over my foot; his wife scolds him, tapping him on the shoulder from behind. I'm barely in the door and already I've lost my mother among pyramids of packaged goods.

I can't get used to a place where furniture comes in boxes and the aisles are like murky streets. I have to skirt a puddle of water appearing out of nowhere like a mirage. Half the shoppers have shaved patches on their scalps revealing parasitic-looking cysts or inflamed scars, as if they escaped from the hospital to convalesce here. Depressed families mope together down the aisles.

When I track down my mother, her cart is filled with twenty-five-pound bags of Super Lucky Elephant rice.

I know the questions I'm supposed to ask: Do you really need this, Mom? Where will you put it? When will you use it? Don't you have something like this already?

Instead, I state the obvious: "Mom, you don't eat rice."

"It's for you."

"What am I going to do with it?"

"You seem like you miss China."

"It would take me about forty years to finish all that. Besides, I don't have anywhere to put it. I moved out of my studio."

She doesn't get all excited and say, "You're leaving Chinatown?" the way my sisters would. She doesn't want to know if I've found an English-speaking job or an English-speaking boyfriend (who is husband material). When my sisters saw my living situation in Oakland, they did not approve. They like to interrogate me then inform me that I'm trying to recreate my life in China, which can only lead to stagnation and despair. "Have you two been reading my diary?" I like to ask them even though I don't keep one.

I help my mother put the rice back on the shelf.

When I returned from China a year ago, my mother brought me here as a kind of celebration, as if to say, Now you can have all the toilet paper and jumbo hot dogs you want! I'd been eating cabbage and rice for the past month, traveling through the smaller towns in Sichuan, circling Chengdu, where my ex-fiancé, Wang Weidong, lived. We'd broken up to get a fresh start, and I was stalling, trying to figure out my next move. Then I called home and heard my mother's teeth chattering over the line; she was shaken up because she'd been robbed. Three days later, I was with her in Costco. I got one whiff of a sample someone was handing out, small chunks of spiral-sliced ham, and nearly threw up.

I called a family meeting later that day because I found out that my mother hadn't been robbed at all; my sisters had taken it upon themselves to clean up her clutter, carting away bags of trash, without telling her, while she was out getting her prescriptions refilled.

I didn't think they had a right. My mother was practically catatonic, staring at an empty corner in the living room where her collection of *Consumer Reports* used to be.

It took only about five minutes for Priscilla, the eldest and bossiest, to turn the meeting around so that it was all about me.

"You know you can't go back," she said.

"That's my decision to make."

"You can't keep calling Wong Dong."

"His name is Weidong."

"Whatever it is!"

"Okay, I'll just call you Prispiss."

"The point is you have to move on."

"We were going to open a teahouse together," I said. "We sang karaoke duets every Friday night."

"But he's marrying someone else," Tanya said, practically whispering. She's the youngest and smallest; people are always asking her to speak up. "You said so yourself."

"He doesn't love her the way he loves me."

Both of my sisters—they should have been twins—rolled their eyes. I knew what they were thinking: that I should never have gone to China for my thirty-sixth birthday, even if I was sick of my job as a property manager and looking for a way out. But they're both married with kids—their careers as a lawyer (Priscilla) and a social worker (Tanya) on hiatus—so they don't understand. It was meant to be a two-week trip but Weidong was the tour guide and I ended up kissing him on Mount Qingcheng on the second-to-last day.

I found a job teaching English and stayed for two years.

"I've been through a lot with him," I said. "It's not like I can just forget about it all."

They didn't have a comeback for that; no one spoke. I'd e-mailed them about being four months pregnant, and then suddenly I wasn't pregnant anymore. But I didn't have a baby either. I'd spared them the details. For all I know, they might have assumed I'd gotten an abortion.

They would be horrified if they could see me now.

My mother is bereft because her cart is empty.

"Fuck it," I say, and help her load it up with a cast aluminum garden crane and a set of wheeled luggage.

Dollar Tree's display window is decorated for all seasons: holiday tinsel, dancing plants, beach balls, and ornamental leaves. So are the people inside: A man wears a ski hat and pajama pants even though it's seventy degrees outside. A woman is dressed in a parka and shorts. Nobody seems to grasp that it is May; I'm guessing Dollar Tree does not sell calendars. I follow my mother down the aisles, watching her toss items into her cart—rain ponchos, nail clippers, pill organizers, foot powder, ant-killer bait trays, air freshener, sunglasses—telling myself I'll put a stop to it when the cart gets half-full. But when she goes for the kitten figurines—eight of them—I lose patience.

"Seriously?" I say. "They look like preemies. They have that wrinkly skin and their eyes are sealed." I lift one up out of her cart and pretend to gag.

My mother examines the one I'm holding and puts them all back on the shelf.

She makes up for it in the party section, where she loads up on army men and rubber reptiles and mechanical pencils for my sisters' kids.

"In some countries," I remind her, "children play with sticks and dead beetles they find outside. They don't have all this stuff, the mounds of toys kids here do."

My mother shrugs her shoulders, no small effort. "We're in America," she says.

"You used to travel," I say, almost accusingly, because from the look of her—the wide swath of her jean skirt, the dumpy giant-sized floral blouse—you'd think she'd never been on a plane. "Does the Luxembourg School of Finance ring a bell? The University of Cambridge? Didn't you and Dad move us to Hong Kong for a semester?"

My mother crumples up her face, the way she does whenever any of us bring up Dad. If you didn't know her, you'd think she was reacting to something she just ate. Nine years later, it's still a major challenge for her to control her grief.

I follow her around a corner, where she stops her cart and hisses: "He doesn't own a cat! He's going to eat that himself!"

She points to a man transferring a stack of Friskies cans into his basket.

And just like that, her whole face lights up in a way I haven't seen since the day she wouldn't stop staring at a tree on campus and my father had to pick her up (she was slim then) and carry her away. She went on medical leave, during which time my father, who was twenty years her senior, died of a heart attack. In the end, she never went back to teaching. There were rumors among her students she'd saved over a million dollars, stashed in small denominations around her house.

"What makes us better than him, Mom?"

"We don't eat cat food!"

"The tuna fish you buy tastes like cat food to me."

But I didn't fly up here to argue, and I'm guessing my mother doesn't need her blood pressure any higher than it already is, so I say, "Look!" and direct her attention to a rack of plastic leis. We try them on. Mine is yellowed, a string of prehistoric teeth. When my mother thinks I'm not looking, she takes every last one—defective or not—and heaps them on top of the sunglasses.

In the checkout line, there's a problem up front. A middle-aged man with a cart full of kitchenware doesn't speak English. He's dressed in a black windbreaker and has the stoic look of a professional ear cleaner in Renmin Park. I make my way towards him when I hear him speak Chinese.

"She says you need five more dollars," I inform him. "Everything costs a dollar each."

He gives me a quizzical look, as if to say: "You're white. We're in America. How on earth are you speaking Chinese?" It's the look I get everywhere except Chinatown, which is part of the reason I've been living there ever since I got back. In Chinatown, people come to me to decipher application forms and financial statements. Most mornings, I find sesame candy and green bean cakes outside my door.

And then I can't help myself: I ramble on to the man about how happy I was in Chengdu, how I loved the music and the art, how Weidong used to wait for me by our favorite noodle stall when I got out of class. I tell him how the baby came too early, frothy and blue, and how, after, Weidong went berserk, reading the birth certificate out loud to strangers and shouting in the streets. I tell the man I think what's happened is my life ended there, but hasn't quite started up here. In the meantime, I have Chinatown—my bakery, the woman who cuts my hair, even the early morning sounds of carts being pushed down the street. I tutor English, sometimes for money, more often not.

My mother stares at me the way she does when I speak Chinese, head cocked, nostrils flared, as if trying to discern if I'm a hologram or the real thing.

Finally, she says, "Okay, Gina, that's enough. I think he gets the point. Tell the nice man goodbye."

"Mothers," I say to him, rolling my eyes.

But he's already got his back to me, counting his change.

"Maybe we should go home," my mother says, back in the car, her facial hair glistening in the midday sun. As far as I can tell, these are the things I have to look forward to with age: furry cheeks, excessive weight gain, and some kind of mental breakdown that will leave me devoid of all emotional attachment except to inanimate, crappy things. I'm thinking the last-mentioned has already happened to me, except that I had the opposite reaction and got rid of everything I owned.

In any case, I can't stand to see my mother so easily defeated.

"Go home?" I scoff. "We're on a mission, Doctor! There's no stopping us now."

"You seem tired."

"Me? Tired?"

"Anyway, it's time for lunch."

As if my mother, weighing in at over two hundred pounds, adheres to a meal schedule.

"Okay, if you're hungry," I say. "We can take a quick break."

The plan—in my mind, at least—is to fuel up on junk food and caffeine and then head back out, but when we pull up to the house, everything is eerily quiet—no chirping birds, not even a mangy squirrel. There's a cracked window; some of the shingles stick out like errant fins. The screen door teeters in the breeze. My first thought: *vandals*! I tell my mother to stay in the car while I get out and inspect. The grass is patchy, the yard infested with weeds. The bushes in front are mottled and overgrown. A wayward branch taps the cracked glass. Cardboard covers the bottom half of the windows.

I walk back to the car. "Something's not right."

"I've done a lousy job of keeping up the place," my mother says. "That's all."

We carry the boxes from Costco and the bags from Dollar Tree to the front door, but it doesn't open all the way, so we can't get them through. I have to squeeze in sideways to assess the situation: the problem appears to be a toppled stack of magazines and a ski pole wedged behind the door. Inside, handwritten diagrams and lists line the walls of the front hall; there are papers—clipped articles, index cards, pamphlets, fliers—piled chest-high. In the dimness of the living room, I can make out a stack of plastic chairs, a birdbath, a bicycle wheel, a chandelier, rolls of wrapping paper, and a wall of Tupperware containers containing—for all I know—nail clippings. A clock radio blinks. To get to the kitchen, you have to follow a narrow path through the junk. There are two large appliance-sized boxes blocking the stairs.

I toss away the fallen magazines, pick up the ski pole, and open the front door. "Mom, where do you sleep?"

She points to the corner of the living room, to a small, uncovered space on a couch, the same couch that used to be on top of her car. "It's getting too hot upstairs anyway."

"You sleep sitting up?"

"One of the perks of getting older."

We add her recent purchases to the stockpile and I follow her along the path to the kitchen. It's like an inverse nature trail through human detritus, a scenic tour of a life gone wrong. In the kitchen, crusty dishes and saliva-smudged glasses sit high in the sink. I pick up a ten-year-old issue of *Gourmet* with a picture of a fruit tart on the front, and my mother, defensive, says, "I'm planning on making that as soon as I have time."

By now, my sisters are probably thinking I've had a heart-to-heart with Mom and come up with a sensible plan to make scheduled donations to Goodwill, but they cleaned out the place a year ago and it's only gotten worse. For whatever reason—security, warmth, companionship—my mother needs to live encased by her junk.

"You'd make a killing on eBay," I venture.

"None of it's for sale."

My mother clears off the kitchen table—moving what I can only identify as a Habitrail on top of the stove—then leaves the room and comes back carrying two plastic chairs and hands me mine. I didn't know it was possible to downgrade from Twinkies—my mother's junk food of choice—until she places a platter of hot dog buns in the middle of the table and provides me with a saucer for a plate. There are no hot dogs, she informs me, but she has every condiment under the sun. I choose hoisin sauce to throw her, but she returns with a duct-taped, red-capped bottle. I sniff it; it seems okay. Another one of my mother's calculations: shelf life. She disdains perishables.

"We're just going to eat them like this?" I say.

"I didn't think you were expecting a three-course meal."

"I wasn't."

"And I ran out of Twinkies. I know they're your favorite."

"Okay," I say, "that's fine."

But it's not, I can tell, because she's staring at me. I take a bite of the bun with the hoisin sauce and my eyes water up. In the midst of the silence, the clock on the wall sounds like a drum.

"Is it true?" she asks.

"Is what true?" I discreetly transfer my bun to my lap and try to remove the sauce with my finger.

The clock pounds away.

"That you live like a bum," she says.

"Says who?" I say, but I don't need to ask. When my sisters saw the dirty bare walls of my studio and my roll-up sleeping mat, they clung to each other like they were visiting me in jail. "Anyway, I'm moving."

"You didn't bring in your bags," my mother says.

"I'll get them after lunch."

"Why don't you get them now?"

"If that will make you happy, Mom," I say, wiping my finger off on the side of the saucer. I try to stay calm so she will too: now would not be a good time for her to have a stroke. I forge my way back out of the house, practically tripping over a test-tube rack, and then plunge back in carrying my bags, when I do trip over the test-tube rack, twisting my ankle.

"Is there some kind of science experiment going on?" I say, limping back into the kitchen.

But she ignores my question, telling me to move the platter of buns—where, I want to ask, should I tape it to the ceiling?—and place my bags on the table before her.

Then she wants me to unpack.

"Don't you have enough stuff, Mom?" I say. "Do you really need some of mine?"

"I only want to look."

"You'll be disappointed."

"Start with the suitcase."

I spring it open. Nothing's inside.

My mother gasps.

"Do you have at least a change of clothes?" Her bottom lip quivers and perspiration seeps from the folds in her neck. Her breath is shallow and there's a lack of focus in her eyes. The color is starting to drain from her face. I know she's going to die sooner than later, maybe any day, maybe right here with me.

That would not go over well with my sisters.

"Mom, you look sick! You need to take your medicine!" I say.

But she shakes her head and motions for me to open my backpack.

It's clear to me the only way we can relate is through my things. So I take them out and hand them to her one by one: from the main compartment, a comb and toothbrush. From a side pocket, the rind of a lychee. From the other side pocket, my money belt and passport and name chop. She takes my belongings, stroking and tapping them, as if scrounging for loose change.

"That's it?" she says. "That's all?"

"It was supposed to be a new beginning for me," I say.

She drops her face into her hands.

"Mom?"

She doesn't respond.

"Mom?"

I can't tell if she's breathing.

"Mom!" I pull out one last thing folded inside a Ziploc and use it to swat the top of her head.

She looks up. "What is it?"

I hold it out to her. "It's got his name and sex and date of—"

"Stop!"

And my mother, who collects bottle caps, and ticket stubs, and coupons, and empty cereal boxes, and plastic utensils, and petrified Twinkies, my mother who—I get it now—is a full-blown hoarder, even she will not touch it. There were days I stared at it for hours, trying to understand, but now I can't bear to look either. My mother turns to face the stove, pivoting her chair.

"We said we were breaking up to forget about the baby," I say to her back, "but part of me wonders if I wasn't Chinese enough for him."

My mother looks at me over her shoulder, sniffs. "You seem plenty Chinese to me."

"I don't have the right disposition. I'm too tall."

"You speak the language beautifully."

"My tones are off."

She stands up and walks away from me, away from disaster, I think, back to the safety of her possessions, but then she lifts a burner off the stove and pulls out a stack of hundred-dollar bills.

She tries to hand me the money, but the muscles in her face, her neck, even her forearms contract, and I know if I take it, she'll just curl up and die. Not because she doesn't have enough—I too believe there's a million dollars hidden around the house—but because this fortress of crap is her soul. She watches me shake my head and her face dissolves into relief.

"They said I should help you," she says.

"God, Mom, don't listen to them."

"They'll be furious if I don't."

"I'll be okay."

"What will you do for work?"

"You sound like Priscilla."

My mother nods. "She told me to ask."

I pick up the burner and help her stuff the money back.

A few weeks later, I'm back in Chinatown, in the same building, in a studio one floor up. I've gotten a job as a bank teller, my Chinese coming in handy yet again. I go to take out the certificate because I need to see where it registers on the scale of this next stage of my life. But it's not there. Did I lose it? I stare at a smudge on the wall, trying not to panic. I imagine my mother sneaking it out of my backpack into one of her piles.

She had once run fifty miles in five hours and forty minutes, but here she was, eight years later, on the chubby side, drinking Chardonnay straight from the bottle, not yet 10 a.m. Her husband, Troy, was at the gym. Their two-year-old son, Joey, was in the tot camp, the main draw of The Royal Palm All-Inclusive Resort. At first, she was only going to drop Joey off for a few hours, but then Troy convinced her to leave him all day: the reason they were taking this luxurious vacation in Mexico—even though they couldn't afford it—was to get a break. The morning's itinerary was for Troy to pick her up on his way from the gym to the pool. At the pool, they would ease into their first full day of relaxation, just the two of them, since Joey was born. Troy had made her promise not to talk about how they were going to pay for it all until after they returned home to Portland. Then, reinvigorated and fresh, they would assess the damage and come up with a plan.

"Heather?" Troy appeared in the doorway of their casita now, his lean arms glistening with sweat. She'd been the one to inspire him to take up running; he'd been a slacker and a lush when they first met.

He saw her holding the open bottle of wine but chose not to comment. It had been in a bucket of ice when they arrived the night before, part of the welcome package—along with baby wipes and teething biscuits—but he didn't touch the stuff anymore. It made him feel sluggish. Instead, he snacked on roasted almonds and kale chips and sipped green tea. It was like they'd reversed roles and he was the one in training, although for what was anybody's guess. Maybe to combat her moodiness, or impending middle age (he was forty-two, she forty-three), or Joey's chronic diarrhea, which smelled terrible and meant they would have to put off potty training until he was four. She took one last swig and set the bottle down.

They walked hand in hand to the pool, where Troy plucked two striped, detergent-scented towels from a pile and spread hers out on a chaise lounge, unaware that this was a job for the staff. He kicked off his flip-flops and clasped his hands above his head. He'd gotten a crew cut for the vacation and it subtracted ten years.

"Nice," he said, scanning the pool.

She nodded, took out her *People* magazine.

"How are you feeling?" he asked.

She could have told him that she felt no different, that the dread was still jammed like a rock down her throat, but there was no sense ruining things at a thousand bucks a day. Wait until they were back home with their leaky faucets, surrounded by fruit flies, sitting in their wobbly, secondhand chairs. Besides, she'd only been on the new dosage for three weeks and the doctor had said to give it five.

"Fine."

"Really?" He removed his shirt, tossed it underhand onto the back of his chaise. He ran his hand along the top of his spiky hair. He was so hopeful—or naive, depending on how you looked at it—that she sometimes wondered how he'd made it this far in life. How had he not been robbed blind or mauled by a bear?

"Going for a swim?" she asked.

"I just might." He stood at the edge of the pool and dipped his toes in the water. She watched him, and desired him, which was good because one of the side effects of the medication was supposed to be lack of libido. Happiness at this stage was proving the medical establishment wrong.

He looked out over the pool, past the cherub spitting water, past the potted palms, past a waiter carrying a tray of slushy pastel drinks, until his gaze rested on a couple playing cards at a table in the shade. The man was in a baseball cap, pale with a paunch. The woman managed to be stylish while wearing a sleeping toddler in a sling. The sight of her made Heather thankful she was not, at this very moment, attending her Baby & Me group back home. She'd been going to meetings out of desperation, hoping the other mothers would, for once, indicate she was doing something right. Waking up in Mexico that morning (and drinking half a bottle of wine) had given her perspective: she was never going back to Baby & Me again.

Troy walked around the rim of the pool until he was standing in front of the couple. The man tipped his baseball cap and looked up.

Immediately he jumped out of his chair, and he and Troy performed what Heather recognized as Troy's old fraternity handshake. It ended with both of them blowing on their fingers to simulate smoking guns. They talked. They jostled each other in a joking, tough-guy manner and compared biceps. (Troy won.) They ran hands through their various degrees of thinning hair. (Troy's not so much.) Then Troy turned and signaled for Heather to join them, but she was saved by a waiter, who arrived in front of her holding out a fruit-laden drink complete with umbrella.

After a few minutes, Troy wandered back and gave her the report: it was his old college buddy, Zach, the one who used to get drunk and hijack the campus recycling truck. Troy hadn't talked to him in years, and here he was. He'd turned out to be an R&D engineer—who would have known! He and his wife, Crystal, had an eighteen-month-old daughter named Fern. He wanted Heather to come meet them.

Heather flipped the page of her *People*. "I don't think so."

Troy looked her over, searching for clues. "Why not?"

Heather indicated the sling, the baby.

"Because they have a kid?" Troy said. "We have a kid."

"I've decided my problem isn't postpartum depression. It's these other mothers. They're killing me. I'm on vacation. Fuck Baby & Me."

Troy twisted his lips to the side the way he did when she reported what he took to be imagined slights. He called her the Queen of Misinterpretation. When she told him about the comments people made when she bottle-fed Joey (Breast is best! Poor thing!), he assumed they said those things out of genuine concern. He couldn't understand why she couldn't just shake it off and go for a jog.

"Zach's a good guy," he said. "I don't think he'd marry anyone like that."

"No one starts out that way. They change when they have a kid."

"She doesn't seem the type."

"They didn't even put their daughter in the tot camp. They're probably doing that attachment-parenting thing. Just tell them I've got whooping cough."

But it was too late because the couple had gotten up and was walking over to them. The baby was awake, face out in the sling. They stopped in front of Heather, blocking her sun.

"When Troy told me he was married to you, I thought he was making it up," Zach said, thrusting out a hand. Heather shook it.

"I used to read all about you," Crystal said. "And I loved those Nike ads." She wore a turquoise sarong with a coral design, costing, Heather guessed, somewhere in the vicinity of her and Troy's monthly rent.

There were the usual questions: Did Heather still hold the fifty- and hundred-mile records? No, both were broken the following year. Where did she keep her medals? In a shoebox in a closet. Was it true she performed CPR on a fellow runner in the middle of the Western States Endurance Run? Yes, but only for twenty-five seconds before the paramedics arrived. And she hadn't won that race, contrary to popular belief. She'd come in second.

"Wow," they both said, "that must have been amazing."

"It was another lifetime," Heather said.

"Do you miss it?" Crystal said. Fern hung there wide-eyed and motionless like an exotic pendant. Heather expected Crystal to wave at her with the baby's hand—or worse, speak for the baby using a squeaky voice—but Crystal merely blinked, waiting for Heather's response.

"Sure I do," Heather said, "but I don't have time to think about it running after Joey." She looked around for him, remembered he wasn't there. "You know, between teaching him French and violin…" She glanced over at Troy; he was not amused.

"You're funny," Crystal said. "I like that. It's nice to meet a parent with a sense of humor."

"He's in the tot camp today. This is the first time—"

"Oh yeah, Fern would be in there if she didn't have a fever. I've got my fingers crossed for tomorrow."

"That's amazing she just sits there like that. Joey would be kicking and biting to get out."

"It's the Tylenol. She isn't normally like this."

Then Heather started laughing, maybe out of relief that Crystal, unlike the other mothers, hadn't brought up potty training or language development in the first minute of their conversation. Not only did Joey crap his diaper all day, he had yet to say a word.

"Hey, do you want to get together for dinner tonight?" Zach said. He'd turned his cap around so it was on backwards. "We could tell the wives some stories from our college days."

"Yeah, if we can remember anything," Troy said. "Weren't we passed out the whole time?"

"Pretty much," Zach said. "Now I'm jonesing for a cigarette."

They made arrangements to meet outside of the grill, the most kid-friendly of the three restaurants at the resort. Troy and Zach high-fived. Heather and Crystal exchanged pleasantries about how much fun it would be, then gave each other little waves.

After the couple left, Heather said, "Dinner?"

"What could I say?" Troy held up his hands.

"That we had plans."

"With whom? Joey and his binky? The consul general?"

"They'll ask us what we do," Heather said.

"I'm a fifth-grade teacher and you're at home with Joey. We work hard. We have no reason to be ashamed."

"Except that we're living beyond our means." She scooped a piece of pineapple out of her drink.

"For this once. This one single vacation. Isn't that what credit cards are for?" He was under the impression if you deserved something enough, the money would fall from the sky.

"Joey's going to scream the whole dinner," she said.

"He doesn't always do that."

"What if he has a blowout?"

"Listen, Zach's solid. And Crystal couldn't be nicer. They have a kid. They'll understand."

"You always say that," Heather said.

For the rest of the morning, they read and swam and collected umbrellas from their drinks. They ate shrimp cocktail by the pool. Back at their casita, Heather painted her toenails while Troy flipped through the resort brochure and read key sections: "'Unwind in the lap of luxury. Let us cater to your every need. Live the way you dream. Watch your dreams become real.'"

"Deep," Heather said.

Troy pretended to be offended, tackled her on the bed. They rolled over each other, removing their clothes.

An hour later, lying with her head on Troy's chest, Heather could feel the guilt creeping in. She'd never left Joey for longer than three hours. That morning, he'd cried and clung to her when she handed him over. She'd had to forcefully peel him off.

"I could get used to this," Troy said, playing with her hair.

"Do you mind if we pick up Joey a little early?" she asked.

At the tot camp, the lights were dim; most of the babies were napping on mats. There was a machine making white noise. A couple of older kids watched cartoons. Joey sat rocking himself in the corner of the room, facing the wall. The caretaker, a young Mexican woman with limited English, tried to explain that he wouldn't let her hold him. She handed them a plastic bag full of Joey's soiled clothes. Heather worried people didn't take to Joey because he had gaunt cheeks and rarely smiled. She walked over and scooped him up.

She'd missed him. He nuzzled his face against hers, slipped his arms through the opening in her collar down the front of her shirt. She was relieved to have him with her again; he was safe. Nothing bad had happened to him while they were apart. She carried him out into the lobby, over the polished tiled floor, feeling the strain in her lower back. Troy lugged the diaper bag in tow and gave her the count: all eight diapers had been used and there were no more spare clothes. As if on cue, a sweet, rank smell began to emanate from Joey. Heather felt a gush of warmth on her hip. Troy grabbed Joey and dodged into a restroom. He came out twenty minutes later with Joey cleaned up but naked from the waist down. He passed Joey to Heather. Heather held Joey on the side of her that was not covered in shit.

At the lobby exit, there was a parrot in a cage. Joey clawed his way out of Heather's arms, nearly removing her shirt in the process. He slid down her body, kicking her shins with his Velcro sandals, then ran and stuck his finger in the cage. The bird bit it. Joey howled. Troy swept him out of the lobby onto a lush expanse of lawn. Heather followed, pointing out the colorful birds flitting through a row of lime trees, but Joey was not consoled. Troy lifted him on his shoulders and ran circles around the lawn, around a tile fountain, until Joey finally stopped crying.

There were other sights that required stopping along the sand path back to their casita: men with rakes, an iguana scurrying beneath a rock, a waterfall trickling down into a pool with lily pads and koi, an intricately carved stone bench. Joey sat down on the bench and held his hand out for a snack. They gave him a baggie of Cheerios; he was going through a Cheerios-only phase. He climbed down from the bench and peed on the ground. They covered it with sand. He tossed the baggie and its contents; they retrieved them. Heather had once run three hundred miles without sleep (another record), but the exhaustion she'd felt after was nothing compared to this.

In their casita, Heather soaked her shirt and Joey's soiled clothes in the bathroom sink. She and Troy shot it out to see who got the first shower. She won. Still, it was hard to relax when there were loud thuds coming from the room, sending seismic vibrations through the bathroom floor. Joey was jumping off the bed. Once he started, it was hard to get him to stop. After her shower, Heather tried to distract Joey by reading him a book, but he grabbed the book out of her hand and threw it across the room. "No, thank you," she told him. "You can say, 'No, thank you.'" But Joey wasn't listening. He was trying to unplug the lamps. "That's dangerous," she said, dragging a chair in front of the outlets. "You could get hurt." Joey tried to move the chair away, but she held it in place. His little arms quivered. He puffed his cheeks with air. Out of protest, he ran around Troy's suitcase and rammed his head into the wall. A swelling began to take shape on his forehead. Heather put him in the Pack 'n Play and went into the bathroom to get a wet towel. By the time she returned, Joey had climbed out.

"Hut," he said.

"What was that?"

"Hut." Joey touched his forehead.

"That's right, you got hurt." Heather stood back; this was the closest they'd ever come to a conversation.

She shouted into the steam of the bathroom: "He just said his first word!"

"What was it?"

"Hurt."

"What?" Troy stepped out of the shower, toweling himself off.

"Hurt, as in, I hurt myself."

"Isn't it supposed to be doggy or something like that?"

Heather shrugged. "I'll take it. It's better than nothing."

Troy held Joey while Heather dabbed at the blood. Then Heather ran after Joey holding a pair of pants. How could she win ultramarathon after ultramarathon but have this much trouble dressing her child? She and Troy had to double up and wrestle him down. Even Troy was breathless, rolling his eyes.

They were late to dinner, of course; since Joey, punctuality had pretty much gone down the drain. Zach and Crystal were waiting for them, sitting in Adirondack chairs outside the glass door to the grill. Crystal was in a strapless dress, holding a golden clutch and bouncing Fern in her lap. Zach wore a sports coat. Even Troy had put on a button-down. Heather was the only one who hadn't made an effort. She couldn't see the point in dressing up only to have her clothes ruined. Heather was carrying Joey face out, away from her body, like he was contaminated. Joey was biting the air.

"What happened?" Crystal said.

At first Heather thought Crystal wanted to know why they were late, but then realized she was looking at Joey's forehead.

"He kind of bumped into a wall."

"Ouch."

Heather set Joey down and gave Troy the "Think fast!" look. Troy passed her the diaper bag and followed Joey to an ornamental pot, where Joey proceeded to put glass pebbles in his mouth. There was always that judgment call, whether to let Joey do something slightly inappropriate or dangerous, or pull him away, causing a scene. While Troy was making this calculation, brow furrowed, Zach—perhaps sensing this—said, "We'll go on in and grab a table."

Troy tried to coax Joey to open his mouth. "Be right there."

As soon as Zach and Crystal disappeared through the door, Troy swept a finger over Joey's tongue, scooping out the pebble. Joey screamed. They did that trick where they tossed him back and forth between themselves to calm him down.

Once inside, a team of waiters in white jackets whisked them to Zach and Crystal's table and produced trays of food for the toddlers. For the next twenty minutes, it was all business: jello cubes and applesauce and chicken strips and French fries and cartoon sippy cups came and went. Little bunny cheesecakes arrived on edible flower beds for dessert. Joey forgot about his Cheerios phase. The toddlers gorged themselves. There were no accidents or temper tantrums or allergic reactions: no one had to apologize or run out of the room. The lights were dimmed and the waiters came around with battery-operated tea lights, the effect of which was to transform the atmosphere from kiddie to romantic. Heather sat transfixed.

Then Troy and Zach strapped on the carriers. The kids willingly got in them, stared at the flickering tea lights, and fell asleep.

It was a miracle.

"Finally, we can talk!" Zach said.

And talk they did. Heather was dreading the job questions, but they never came. Instead, Zach jumped right in, saying, "Are you guys tired? I mean, I've never felt so tired in my life!"

"All I want," Crystal said, "is to fall into a coma. Hook me up to an IV."

Heather acknowledged she hadn't slept since she was pregnant. Troy, who'd been known, pre-fatherhood, to pass out for twelve hours at a stretch, woke up several times a night because he had a recurring dream about forgetting Joey at Trader Joe's, in a cart in the parking lot. This led Zach to admit that one time, in fact, he had left Fern behind, at the doctor's office, no less. Only for a minute, but still. Troy mentioned the time he went to work wearing Joey's bib, which he put on in the mornings while feeding Joey to protect his shirt from the splatter. It was the principal, passing him in the hallway, who asked him to take it off. Crystal once left the house with a mud mask on her face, but luckily checked herself in the rearview mirror of her car. Zach spent half his days searching for his keys. Troy thought he was losing his sense of humor. Crystal's tailbone still hurt from the birth. Heather confessed she lay awake at night feeling inadequate as a parent. "Jesus, what's happening to us?" Zach said. "We need to bring back the good times!"

Troy announced he couldn't drink anymore, then said, "What the hell," and ordered a pitcher of beer. Crystal and Heather got a bottle of Pinot Noir. Zach and Troy swapped more stories of bungled parenthood: the time Fern swallowed a wad of dental floss while Zach was busy filming her with his iPad (thus proving the whole technology/accident theory), the time Troy held Joey up like an airplane and Joey spit up into Troy's mouth. Heather laughed. This had to be the first time since Joey was born that she had sat unencumbered in a beautiful restaurant with other like-minded adults, having a good time. She could smell the grilled steak from the buffet. Joey's head rolled back: he was out for the night. Heather excused herself to go to the restroom, not to get away, but to indulge in the freedom and good fortune of the moment.

It was a luxury to use the restroom by herself. Often Joey unraveled (and ate) the toilet paper or she had to somehow secure him while squatting over the seat. But tonight, she examined a splotch on her cheek in the mirror, taking her time. The wine felt warm in her stomach; there was color in her cheeks. She wished she'd worn a dress. If they ever had the money, this was how she wanted her bathroom to look back home. The sinks were hand-painted. A stalk of jasmine perfumed the air. It was an oasis. She washed her hands, inhaling the lavender-scented soap. It felt like the meds were finally starting to kick in. It would get easier; it had to. People were always telling her how quickly it went by. Before she knew it, Joey would be taking the school bus; she'd get back into shape, maybe start her own business as a trainer. Until then, she just needed a night like this every once in a while.

The door of the restroom swung open. For a second Heather thought it was Troy coming to tell her that Joey had woken up screaming and they had to cut the evening short, but it was Crystal, herself empty-handed. She appeared to have come to the bathroom for the sole purpose of applying lipgloss. The two of them stood side by side at the sinks.

"I wanted to tell you how much I respect you," Crystal said, sliding the lipgloss back into her glittery purse. She seemed nervous, perhaps a little star-struck. "It must be so hard."

Heather had heard it before: her world-famous training regimen made Michael Phelps look like a slacker. She'd been on the covers of *Ultrarunning* and *Running Times* magazines. In a Nike commercial that aired during the Super Bowl, she'd run against a cheetah, passing it three hours and ten minutes into the race. There'd been a reality show in which beefy male athletes tried to keep up with her and failed. In an interview with Oprah, she'd once said, "The fun doesn't start until mile sixty, and I'm all about having fun." After fifty-mile ultras, she'd been known to jog back to her hotel. But that was a long time ago. People couldn't understand that she'd stopped all of that for good.

"If you only knew how out of shape I am. I couldn't even tell you the last time I put on a pair of sneakers."

"No, I mean what you're doing now," Crystal said, dabbing her lips with a tissue. "Choosing to take care of Joey. That's pretty heroic."

"In all honesty, it's not like I gave anything up. I was slowing down. Everyone had a different theory why but the point is I began to suck. I would have retired anyway. I tried working in sales, in athletic apparel, but it just didn't hold my interest."

"But still, I mean, some parents completely freak out or shut down. Did you have any kind of training?"

Heather watched Crystal ball up the tissue and drop it in the trash. "I'm not sure what you mean."

"My sister's kid has something similar and everyone is yelling and screaming all the time. It's like the whole family's gone crazy. You guys are sane."

"Is something wrong with your sister's kid?"

"Listen, it's none of my business really. It's just a long-winded way of saying I admire you, that's all."

"Excuse me." Heather brushed by Crystal and exited the restroom.

At the table, Troy and Zach were nursing their beers, smoking cigarettes, sleeping toddlers be damned.

"Where'd you get those?" Heather said.

"Bummed them off a waiter."

"Troy, can I talk to you for a minute? Outside?"

"Okay, but first I'd like to give you fair warning that Zach and I are planning to steal a couple of those white jackets and impersonate hotel staff, maybe check out the stables and get in a little horseback riding, which, as you may know, is *not* included in the price of this all-inclusive resort. In fact, it's like an extra four hundred bucks a day. Which we don't have. Because, unlike Zach, and Crystal, who has her own fashion line, we chose the wrong careers. So if you wake up tomorrow morning and can't find me, there's a chance I'm being held for questioning." He licked the beer off his lips, took a drag, and leaned back in his chair.

"Way to summarize," Zach said. "Could you explain all that to Crystal too?"

"I'll be waiting for you around back," Heather said.

Outside the grill, standing on a balcony overlooking the lit-up pool, Troy said, "What happened this time?" His voice was hoarse, the way it got when he drank. "Did someone comment on Joey's baby acne, try to slip you a bottle of Oxy 10? Or was it Joey's male pattern baldness, which makes him look creepy and distinguished at the same time? We could get him a toupee, but don't come running to me when he hangs upside down off the monkey bars." He was on a roll, the way he'd been when he'd first introduced himself to Heather after the Kamikaze One Hundred, at a post-race beer festival. He'd told her he'd dressed up as her for Halloween, his beer gut hanging out between tank top and shorts. He'd never jogged a day in his life.

"It's Crystal," she hissed. She was seething: even worse than the judgmental mothers were the ones who appeared to be open-minded and then caught you off guard in the restroom.

"Okay," Troy said. "I'm listening."

"She thinks something is wrong with Joey."

"What exactly did she say?"

"She compared Joey to her sister's kid who apparently has a serious problem." She looked at Troy, expecting him to twist his lips in dis-belief. She waited for him to tell her it was all a misunderstanding, to mock her with his scrunched-up imitation of her anxious face. Troy readjusted Joey's head and kissed him.

"Oh God, Heather."

"You think I'm overreacting?"

"I wanted to tell you."

"I know, I need to lighten up."

"The other week, I was with Joey at the park and a plane flew overhead—it was loud—and every single kid looked up except Joey."

She stared at Troy. This was completely unlike him. "So he needs to get his hearing checked?"

"I'm pretty sure his hearing is fine."

"He could have thought the noise was coming from a truck."

Troy hitched up the carrier and tightened the belt. "I'm starting to get this feeling in my gut that something's wrong with him. Maybe that's why it's so hard for you, for us."

"Oh, so now it's you and Crystal."

"We'll just explain to the doctor."

"But he said his first word."

"I know. It might be nothing. I could be wrong."

She turned her back on him; it felt like he'd sucker-punched her in the throat and dislodged the rock, releasing the dread to course through her body, up to her scalp, down her legs.

"We're going to figure this out together, okay?" he said.

She whipped around, planning to face him, but instead fixed her eyes on Joey's feet, his bony little crisscrossed toes. "No, it's not okay. You can take Joey to the doctor yourself—or better yet, why don't you and Crystal go?—because I'm done. He's all yours."

She stormed up the perfectly manicured sand path. She felt ridiculous. She hadn't done this since the third grade. Plus, she was out of shape. Troy easily caught up.

He cut in front of her, turned and blocked her way. "You're talking crazy," he said.

"That's me, your crazy wife."

"The medicine's not working, is it?"

She didn't answer; she had a sudden urge. She unstrapped her sandals, handed them to him. "I'm off," she said, and sprinted up the path, past the gym and spa, around a small orchard, over the spongy grass of the putting green. By the time she reached the tennis courts, she was sucking wind. The urge passed.

Why run when you could walk? Why walk when you could lie in a ditch? She flopped down by the side of an ornamental pond. Frogs cheeped. She looked at her watch. When enough time had passed, she mucked up her feet and pinched her cheeks. She took dew from the grass and rubbed it in her hair. She walked the thirty or so yards back to their casita. Her heart was pounding in her throat; she didn't have to fake that. The door was ajar; she stepped inside. Joey was asleep in the Pack 'n Play, knees tucked, butt in the air. She was going to ask Troy if she should check Joey's diaper, but he was on the phone. Her bottle of wine was in the trash. The room was cleaned out, bags packed and piled by the door, as if they'd never been there, as if they should have known better than to come.

On the two-hour boat ride out to T— Island, my father stood addressing a group of tourists. There were five of them, in baseball caps and fanny packs, huddled under a strung-up tarp to stay out of the sun. They swigged bottled water and—out of boredom—rationed a box of saltines. I sat at the opposite end of the boat, on a burlap sack, no hat, scalp ablaze; all I could hear was the rumble of the motor and the waves lapping the sides. I watched my father raise his arms and drop them, his lips moving in silence.

A few months earlier, he'd retired from Buford College, where he taught *Mythical Beasts of the Middle Ages* over and over again for thirty-five years. Still, he wore his teaching outfit: a tweed jacket and an antique ring with the family crest. He had a beard that, unmitigated by reading glasses, gave you the impression he'd just come from hauling wood. He'd always loved to lecture, and what better audience than one captive on a small wooden boat? His audience gazed past him towards the island ahead looming up from the fog. I knew how they felt; I'd had to listen to him for years.

The captain, a brown-toothed man in frayed denim shorts, cut the engine and gave everyone the thumbs-up. He motioned for his assistant, an adolescent version of himself, to pull in a red buoy resembling a playground ball.

It was then with the motor quiet that I heard my father say, almost shout, "We've come here for the dragons!" He held his binoculars dramatically poised in midair.

One tourist coughed. Another opened his *Go Asia!* guidebook. I rolled my eyes. Ahead, the outline of jagged mountains and jungle came into view.

He meant, of course, the lizards. But I was tired of rescuing him, of doing all the explaining. In the past month alone, I'd taken him to the emergency room three times, twice for premature ventricular contractions, and most recently for a gout attack that made his foot swell to twice its size. I'd filled out paperwork and met with doctors until I knew his symptoms and vital signs by heart.

The captain and his assistant leaned over the side of the boat, over a makeshift wooden railing. The boy maneuvered a pole with a hook at the end, trying to snag the buoy.

"Let's take a gander here," my father said, still using his classroom voice, wedging himself in between the captain and the boy. Next to them, he looked ridiculously overdressed, as if he'd come all this way to receive an award. He leaned against the railing and announced, "It appears to be a trap of some sort. Lobster? Crab?" He removed his jacket, flung it on top of the luggage, and guided the boy: "A little to the left, farther out now, almost there."

I should have been on the alert considering his recent ER record, but I was reluctant to get up from my warm burlap sack. By the time I made my way over, the railing had collapsed and he had fallen overboard. The captain grabbed an orange lifesaver and tossed it to him. Together, we reeled my father in, grasping him under the arms and pulling him up over the side. He lay on his back and coughed. The other tourists gathered around like gawkers at a roadside accident.

I knelt down beside him. "Are you trying to force me into a career in emergency medicine?"

"No, but you'd make a good doctor, Joan. You have the right instincts."

The second greatest sorrow of my father's life was that, at the age of thirty-two, I was tending bar.

After his last visit to the ER, his enlarged foot encased in something suited to an elephant, I helped him through the door of his townhouse in Northeast Portland. I hadn't been inside in years—I always picked him up and dropped him off out front, going no further than the stone patio, to avoid seeing his living-room shrine to my mother, who'd moved to France and been out of our lives since I was two. But that day he was jacked up on prednisone, and his elephant shoe thumped like a piano being dragged upstairs, so I put on my imaginary blinders and, guided by the worn path on his shag carpet, delivered him to his bedroom. Then, head still down, I went in search of a pillow to prop up his foot—doctor's orders.

It was in searching for the pillow that I noticed the state of things: his place had the usual feel of a pawnshop—bronze figurines, heavy tapestries, a wall-mounted kite shield with the family coat of arms—but there was the addition of twenty or so empty Chinese takeout cartons strewn about. He'd stacked his mail—unopened—in small rodent piles against the wall. One of the letters was stamped OVERDUE in red. I dared to glance up at the shrine: her starfish earrings were still in the seashell ashtray, but the pictures had been reordered with the one of her wearing his striped bathrobe, raising a glass of champagne, front and center.

Bad sign.

I circled back to the door of his bedroom.

"When's the last time you left your house?" I said, handing him a couple of important-looking bills, including the one stamped OVERDUE.

He put on his reading glasses, skimmed the envelopes with a scholarly air. "Today."

"I mean, besides our excursions to the hospital."

"How else would I eat?"

I held up a takeout box. "You need to get out."

My concern was: if he was moping around his townhouse with nothing to do, then he was obsessing over my mother. If he was obsessing over my mother, pretty soon he'd convince himself that it was all a huge misunderstanding and she missed us terribly and was coming back. This had happened twice before, once when I was ten and had a high fever for a week and went into convulsions (and as a result lost all hearing in one ear), and again when I went off to Amherst, leaving him—his word—bereft. Both times, he wrote her long, passionate pleas. Both times, they went unanswered. Afterwards, there was the toll of disappointment, lasting, give or take, three years. Each time, it fell to me to set him back on his feet.

The phone rang. We let the answering machine pick up. It was the Dean of Faculty's office at Buford, calling to see if he'd received the invitation for the upcoming faculty emeritus luncheon. At my father's last faculty luncheon, which I'd attended, they'd called him up to the podium and presented him with a check. At the time, it had seemed like a pathetic gesture, my father fumbling the microphone, then opting to talk without. The younger faculty had been more interested in poking their breaded chicken fillets than listening to his muted farewell speech. Now it seemed like my only hope.

"What about that grant they gave you to travel?" I said, as soon as the machine clicked off.

My father motioned to his foot, rapped the casing with his knuckle.

So I spoke of *The Hunt of the Unicorn* and symbolism in heraldry, regurgitating boring old dinner topics I was sure I'd forget. I reminded him of his replacement at Buford—Columbia hotshot, wearer of black turtlenecks, YouTube aficionado—who scoffed at these very things.

He looked up; I'd hit a nerve.

I continued. "I mean, who's going to do the research if not you? I heard Mr. YouTube is a fan of *Harry Potter*. His students are required to bring tablets—you know, mobile computers—to class."

This hit a bigger nerve: my father equated technology with the fall of mankind.

A few days later, he called me at my apartment, a studio above a tattoo parlor on the seedier side of town. The swelling in his foot had gone down and he wanted to travel to a small island off of Malaysia, where he'd read a species of large lizards were revered as living dragons. It was a long trip but he had it figured out.

"We can fly to Singapore, take a bus from Johor Bahru to Mersing, then hop on a boat," he said.

"We?"

"I'm not sure I can do this on my own." He hadn't done much traveling before; he'd stayed home every evening of my childhood to have dinner with me.

He caught me on a morning when I was feeling hungover and pissed off at my drunk boss for trying to fix me up with his drunk friend.

I agreed to go.

As the boat neared shore, I retrieved a towel from my father's wheeled suitcase. He took it and wiped his neck and beard. I asked him if he wanted to change his clothes, but he touched his button-down and told me it was nearly dry, a testament to the strength of the tropical sun. He sat up as we approached the dock, and I gave him a hand to help him stand. In addition to his suitcase, he'd brought a briefcase full of papers, as if at any moment he might need to cite a reference. I'd brought a backpack containing a daypack stuffed with dirty laundry. The sky was fringed with pink and echoed thunder; the captain informed us, thumbs up, that it was a regular evening occurrence. When the boat reached the dock, the captain's assistant presented my father with his tweed jacket, and my father accepted it with both hands.

"Fellow travelers," my father said, saluting the other passengers on the boat, "it's been a pleasure. Many thanks for your kindness and concern."

"See ya," I said to no one in particular, tossing my backpack ahead of me onto the dock. My scalp prickled in the sun. The captain and the boy heaved my father's suitcase over the side.

My father and I disembarked and stood at the end of a long, narrow dock. He clutched his briefcase, raised his chin, and inhaled, savoring our arrival. The boat motored off with the rest of the passengers to a village with nightlife several beaches away. Impatient, I walked on down the dock. I could hear the wheels of his suitcase behind me catching in the grooves. If they got stuck, he'd breathe heavily and yank. When there was a screeching sound, I turned around to see him raise a finger and proclaim, "Bats!"

On the plane over, he'd told me all about T— Island, the twenty-seven species of mammals, the volcanic rock, the primary jungle. The island was forty-three nautical miles off the port of Mersing in the South China Sea, thirty-eight kilometers long and nineteen kilometers wide. Due to its isolation from the mainland, much of the plant life was unique. The lizards—a type of monitor indigenous to the island—grew up to nine feet long. I'd worn headphones, nodding when it seemed appropriate. After we landed in Singapore, he made me promise to put them away, along with any other "gadgets," for the rest of the trip. "Then what will I do the whole time?" I said to annoy him.

We stepped off the dock, onto a narrow concrete path bordered by thick tangled brush and coconut trees, my father straining to keep up. Part of me wanted to run ahead, to ditch the woodsman with the rolling suitcase, but the other part knew without me he'd never find his post-retirement sense of purpose. Without a sense of purpose, he was prone to fancy, confusing history with the present day. So we were going to find these lizards and call them dragons and this would be his new area of focus. Then there would be no reason for him to write my mother, and I could stop playing doctor and stay away from his townhouse for another five years.

Around a curve, there was something lying across the concrete path. It lumbered into the brush as we got close. I thought I saw a tail whip from side to side.

"Dad!" I said.

"Did you see that?"

"I saw it."

He reached for the small memo pad in his jacket pocket, then froze in place when he realized it wasn't there. He closed his eyes, as if contemplating the magnitude of loss.

"It probably fell out on the boat. You can use mine." He'd bought double of everything for the trip, one for him, one for me.

He stared up at the sky, now purple, and received my offering with pressed lips. Together, we described what we saw—something large, something dark, something saurian—and he wrote it down. "That was no alligator," he said, and to lift his spirits, I answered, "It certainly was not." He stared at the thicket where the thing had disappeared. When we heard the sound of a breaking twig, he looked at me, raising his eyebrows.

"Astonishing," he finally said. He stamped his foot, tugged at a dangling vine. "Indeed, this is real."

"Indeed, Dad?" I felt it my duty to call him on his outdated diction to ease his transition into the real, non-Buford world.

"You know what I mean. You graduated summa cum laude in English."

"And look where it got me."

"You haven't found your passion, that's all."

When we arrived at ABC Chalets, a man in knockoff Ray-Bans led us up a hill, past an outdoor shower made of corrugated aluminum, around the outhouses, to a wooden hut. He removed the padlock, pointed to the mosquito nets and lantern inside, and flipped us the key.

"We just saw something," my father said, wrestling his suitcase up the splintery steps and inside the door. He measured out half the length of the room.

The man lowered his sunglasses to look at us. "That is giant lizard-dragon."

"Yes, dragon!" my father said, delighted to hear someone else use the word.

"Well, it looks like we've come to the right place," I said. I wanted him to have this trip and get back on track with his life so I could get on with mine.

My father nodded vigorously.

The man stood there, expressionless, then smiled. "One time they steal old man from village."

"Good God!" my father said, writing this information down in his memo pad, squinting in the waning light.

The man winked at me, but I ignored him, adding, "Yikes."

The hut was a basic one-room A-frame with angles so steep, we had to duck our heads. The guests before us had gone crazy with candles, covering the place in little volcanoes of melted wax. On the ceiling, spotted geckos stared down at us with wide eyes.

"Man-eater," the man said, following my gaze and pointing to the largest one, about six inches long, perched upside down on a knotted beam. He fanned his hand at us and laughed. "No, no, all friendly." He lit the lantern with a Zippo and left.

My father took out two flashlights from the front pocket of his suitcase and placed them head down on the floor in between the cots. He unraveled cellophane wrap from two bottles of sunblock. Finally, he unzipped an inner compartment and pulled out a travel alarm clock and the picture of her in the bathrobe. He sat down on a cot, placed the picture on his knee. She seemed to be mocking us, toasting our stupidity for traveling thousands of miles in search of an animal we could find at the local zoo.

"That needs to go back inside your suitcase," I said.

"What?" He picked up his alarm clock, wound it.

"Her. Or else I'm taking out my iPad…" It was a bluff; if I was online, it was mostly to Google his latest symptoms.

"O.K.," he said, tucking the picture back inside the inner compartment, but he continued to stare at it through the nylon flap.

My scalp was throbbing by this point, but I managed to say, "Tell me about the monitors," to get his mind into the present and out of the past.

He produced a manila file and briefed me. They were diurnal and semiaquatic. They could climb trees. They'd been known to take down large animals, such as monkeys or deer. If threatened, they inflated themselves with air and expelled this air with a hiss.

"What about their claws?" I knew if he'd brought my mother's picture, then he had probably brought his letters. He'd read them out loud to me numerous times before, and it was torture.

He stood up, hitting his head on the slanted ceiling. It had been a while since I'd asked him a question, or at least one that he wanted to hear.

"Long and sharp! They can tear apart prey! What else would you like to know?"

The next morning, we ate ramen noodles on the steps of our chalet while examining a map of the island. I followed him past yards with chickens, through a small village of twelve or so wooden huts, and onto a jungle path. For hours, I watched his tan, wrinkled pants flap against his calves. He took turns carrying his briefcase in one hand then the other, pointing out kingfishers and trees growing large, thorny fruits. He joyfully explained to me that they were called durians, and that it was illegal—due to their strong odor—to carry them on the subway in Singapore. He'd read that in a journal somewhere.

We walked alongside electricity poles traversing the island, and whenever there was a pole close enough to the path, he tapped it. We looked behind decaying logs and peered up into trees. When we weren't sure which direction to take, he had me sit and wait on a stump while he scouted the area. Other times, he bounded up the path after an exotic-looking butterfly, or cocked his head and squinted at the call of a certain bird. He examined kaleidoscopic fungi and checked the ground for tracks. When we passed a waterfall, he stopped to splash his beard. If there was bushwhacking to be done, he forged ahead.

He remained cheerful even when we returned to our hut that evening having seen nothing more reptilian than a giant millipede. Over noodles—fried this time, courtesy of the chalet kitchen—he explained we needed to change our tactics.

"We?" I said.

"With all of the advances we've made, we're still being outwitted by a creature unchanged since the time of dinosaurs." This appeared to bring him joy.

He surmised if they had survived as long as they had, they were versatile, and had probably learned to hide in the undergrowth of the jungle. Perhaps they were stealthier than he'd originally anticipated. Going forward, we would tread lightly and refrain from applying mosquito repellent. They wouldn't be able to hear us approach or smell us each time they flicked their forked tongues, a motion, he said, that hearkened back to fire-spitting dragons.

"Hearkened, Dad? You're going to need a translator if you keep talking like that."

"You understand me perfectly well."

On the second day—not a lizard in sight—we stopped for lunch at a hut that marked the halfway point across the island. The place was designated as a shop on my father's map, but it was abandoned, and something—some insect—had been feasting on it, eating in random zigzags, as if drunk. We sat with our backs against the boarded-up door, my father situating himself on the side of my good ear. There was a sense of letdown; I'd been hoping for a Coke. He licked his lips, parched, and unpacked a plastic container of curry vegetables and rice. He set it between us, suggesting if we waited long enough, an unsuspecting lizard might come ambling along.

"Damn, I wanted a soft drink," he said.

"Me too."

He leaned his head back and closed his eyes. "Now that I'm retired, maybe this will be my new calling."

"Now you're talking," I said, picturing him traveling often, sending me postcards from distant lands. Maybe he'd lose the jacket, pick up slang. I wouldn't have to be his shuttle service to the ER.

He dozed off with plastic fork in hand. I watched a group of ants gather and form, preparing to raid our curry. Each time I obstructed them, using twigs and leaves, they'd regroup. I splashed them with the warm, metallic water from my canteen; they persevered. My father's eyes jerked open.

"Bartending isn't a career," he said.

"What about *America's Greatest Bartender?*"

"Who's that?"

"It's a show, Dad. It's on something called TV. A bunch of guys chuck glasses in the air while carving lime wedges into tropical flowers behind their backs."

"But does that offer opportunities for growth and exploration? Do they feel the joy of achievement, the thrill of earned success?"

"It's a different kind of satisfaction," I said.

We didn't throw glasses at The Underground, where I worked; people spoke in hushed voices and came and left alone. I'd developed a reputation as someone who listened without judgment, who took away your sorrow and gave you back a beer, so patrons made their way down the cement steps to me for counsel (I used a Buddhist approach: don't get emotional, don't get attached), waiting their turn, leaving what they could spare, usually a couple of bucks, as tip.

"Would it be different..." He hesitated, but I knew what he was going to say. He was forever thinking back to an incident in which I called him crying from a sleepover party in seventh grade and asked him to come pick me up. There'd been music, a game of Truth or Dare, and laughter, all of which my hearing-impaired brain jumbled into a high-pitched roar. Since then, I steered clear of social gatherings.

"I don't know."

"In the right kind of environment you could find meaningful work. Any employer would snap you up."

It was true I could get hired easily enough—office manager, program coordinator—but then what happened was my enthusiasm waned. My lack of enthusiasm tended to take a toll on overall employee morale. After a week or two, I'd be called into my supervisor's office where, after being let go, I'd be the most enthusiastic and hopeful I'd been since the interview.

Then I'd return to The Underground, where dispassion was my best asset.

My father took a few stabs at the curry. I said, "Nothing doing." The wind blew; a prickly pod dropped from a tree.

When the early evening thunder began to echo around the island, we retraced our steps back to our hut.

The following morning, my father woke up with a swollen knee and was having trouble making a fist with his right hand. He'd developed a flurry of bites across his forehead because his mosquito net had holes. The curry we'd eaten the day before wasn't agreeing with his stomach. I nodded at his list of complaints, duly recognizing we were back on that runaway train headed straight to the ER. So I suggested we take the path to the boat dock, only a five-minute walk away, where we first thought we'd seen a lizard on arrival.

"Why didn't we think of that before!" I said, trying to muster up excitement. It sounded like a line from bad TV, but he was too distracted to notice: he was looking in a wooden hand mirror, assessing the bites on his forehead, trying to decide if he was having an allergic reaction.

"They probably wait in the brush watching people walk by," I said, creating dramatic inflection in my voice. It felt weird.

He lowered his hand mirror. "O.K.," he said, "this time you lead the way."

He followed me—briefcase in hand—down the steps of our chalet, down the hill, and onto the concrete path, where I made a show of picking up dried-out pieces of coconut shell and examining them for clues. When the wind blew, I licked my finger, held it up, and said, "East." A thick black ball of animal hair rolled past us in the breeze and I theatrically dodged it. He huffed obediently behind. I scratched the trunk of a coconut tree, examined a fallen leaf, and said, "Pinnate, I believe." From the silence behind, I guessed he was unimpressed. "Do you think we should carry sticks for protection?" I said, upping the charade and, if truth be told, enjoying it. I picked a piece of skin off my peeling scalp and said, "Hey, I'm molting just like them. They molt, right?" But when I turned around he was lying on his back across the path.

My first thought was that I was in no mood to memorize his symptoms in Malay and play interpreter on top of nurse, but then he stamped his feet and kicked them up like a kid having a tantrum.

"Dad?" I said.

"My heart."

"It's a PVC, remember? They're harmless. You have no underlying conditions. They did all the tests."

"Oh, those idiotic machines."

A couple of travelers in neon bandanas and boardshorts walked up the path and stopped in front of him. "Everything all right, mate?" One of them lit a cigarette and offered it up.

"Just my fate on the line, that's all," my father said, accepting the cigarette. He rolled to the side to let them pass.

I stood over him for a minute, then gave up and sat down, wedging my daypack against my lower back. I could hear "Redemption Song" coming from a nearby tourist restaurant, and for his benefit, said, "Bob Marley. This is reggae music."

He took a drag without inhaling.

"You don't smoke, Dad," I said.

"Maybe now's the time to start."

If I leaned forward, I could make out the restaurant, a thatched hut with a few rickety wooden tables and mismatched chairs. I stretched out my legs and felt the burn of the concrete against my calves. I watched a trail of ants make work of an overturned beetle. After we'd heard the same song three times over, I turned to him and said, "Why don't we break for a nice cold beer?"

A beer turned into two, following which the bartender, a blond American with dreadlocks to his waist, served us a local drink fermented from palm-tree sap. The stuff was yellow and smelled like something you'd use to mop a floor. My father swirled his around and took small sips; I downed mine. When the bartender came back to give us refills, my father complained of his intestinal problems. The bartender drew an invisible X over his chest and promised a couple more swigs would kill the bug dead.

Finally, after my father finished his third cup, after the music came to a garbled halt, he pushed back his chair and said, "If only your mother were here."

This was the conversation I'd been hoping to avoid, the one we'd had so many times before, it had started to feel like our theme song, my father doing the singing and me mostly trying to contain myself, halfheartedly humming along.

"What would she do?" I said. "Bake us a pie? Darn our socks?"

He opened his briefcase and rifled through documents until he reached carbon copies of three letters—you'd think he'd never heard of a Xerox machine. Two he had written to my mother previously; the third was new. What struck me then was how predictable parents are, how I could have bet a million dollars he would write my mother again, and how I could have bet the same he'd want to read me his latest installment.

He smoothed the newest letter out on the table between us. "I sent this to her three weeks ago asking for advice."

"How naive can you be, Dad? Do you really think she's ever going to write back?"

He raised his finger and read, "'All along I assumed her isolation was due to her hearing loss, but the fact of the matter is—loss or no—she is a skilled and attentive listener. I have tried to attribute her apathy to the rise of technology and the disengagement of her generation, but her basic lack of curiosity with the world leads me to believe it is something more. If it is a parent's duty to teach his child to find value in life, then I have failed, and now I—.'"

"You'll have to post that on Facebook," I said. "No one reads snail mail anymore."

It was a low blow—my father feared losing everything, namely me, to a vapid virtual world—but he calmly answered, "Apparently your mother does."

"And how would you know that? Did she call? Drop in to say hi?"

He extracted a thick cream-white envelope, the old-fashioned kind, with blue cursive, from his briefcase. "This time she replied."

I reminded myself that happiness is transient and permanence illusory—patrons at The Underground ate this stuff up and came back for more—but I didn't know how to apply it to this particular situation.

"I haven't opened it," he said, smelling the envelope.

I stood up. Truth was: I felt betrayed. I had no memory of her; for the last thirty years it had been my father and me. I excused myself from the table, saying I wanted no part of it, and that when I returned, I expected it to be gone.

I wandered in search of the restroom. The bartender, untangling audiotape from a cassette player, used his elbow to direct me to the back door. Outside, a boy chopping meat motioned to an outhouse with a sheet of plywood for a door.

The boy threw pieces of bone and entrails over his shoulder, over a small bluff. I heard splashes coming from below.

"What's that?" I asked, as the stench of human feces hit me.

"Big lizard," the boy said, and laughed. I moved closer to the edge to see. Eight feet below, in a pool of stagnant water, a pack of alligator-sized lizards climbed over each other, flicking their tongues. The boy went into the kitchen and returned carrying a stack of dirty dishes. He scraped the leftovers from the plates into a bucket and dumped the contents over the side, pouring noodles and rice on top of the lizards. They jerked around, eating food off each other's heads and backs. The water was about a foot deep, rank and oily. Broken chairs and rusty pipes poked out like skeletal trees; plastic jugs and toilet paper bobbed at the edge. The lizards waited on the bank below, listless and rheumy-eyed, no more regal than your average pigeon.

"Dirty garbage," the boy said, throwing a silver soda can over the edge. The stench was so bad my nostrils stung.

Then a fly started attacking me, and my eyes were tearing up, and my father was standing beside me saying, "Excellent work."

"It's a fucking shithole," I said.

He sliced open my mother's letter, and I thought, Seriously? You're going to read it to me now? While I'm standing on top of a sewer? With snot running down my face? And did you really bring your embossed letter opener all this way? Why not pack the family shield? I made it clear in no uncertain terms that if he read the thing, I was going to jump.

But then I thought, Look at him in his musty tweed jacket, wielding his obsolete letter opener: he's the only family I have and he's on his way out. Why not let him have his day? Why stand in the way of the moment he's been waiting for half his life?

I backed off the edge and he hesitantly stepped forward. He held his arm up, dangling the letter, then dropped it into a flurry of teeth and claws.

It was a terrible way to think, but Robert couldn't help it: his son, Nick, had gotten what he deserved. Nick—who'd been scared of the water until he was eleven years old—had been in a surfing accident, fracturing four ribs and puncturing an eye. He was laid up in a community hospital in Hawaii, where he was being monitored around the clock. The doctors didn't know if the eye could be saved. Robert had learned about it from Nick's latest girlfriend, who'd called him at the office, interrupting his presentation on tax and estate planning to a group of high-net-worth clients. She wasn't pleasant or rude, just to the point. As a result, here he was, Robert, the father, on a plane to Kona to deal with the logistics, pay off the debts, once again cleaning up his son's mess.

Ever since graduating from Brown, Nick had made it his mission to be near a beach. In his twenties, he'd lived in a tent, then a yurt, then out of a car, scraping by with odd jobs that, he'd told Robert, allowed him to maximize his time on the board. He'd lived everywhere from Goa, India to Bridgehampton, New York, moving on when the weather turned or the mood struck. He prided himself on being a modern nomad. What exactly he did with his spare time, Robert never knew. Robert was a private banker. He spent his days—and evenings—eating takeout and growing people's assets. He couldn't remember the last time he'd been to the ocean. Nick—perhaps to spite his father—had never opened a bank account or used a credit card. He couldn't have written a check to save his life.

Robert hadn't spoken to Nick since the previous year, when Nick had come to New York for his mother's wedding and met Robert at a coffee shop. Nick claimed Robert's apartment, with its upholstered chairs and silver change dishes, all its *stuff*, made him uncomfortable.

So Robert had picked a no-frills coffee shop off of Lexington Avenue, where the sullen barista had a nose ring, in large part because his ex-wife's upcoming wedding was looming over him and he wanted to call a truce with his son. Robert arrived early and carried his coffee to a corner table, promising himself to stay calm, exchange pleasantries, and have a nice quiet chat in which all judgment was withheld. His ex-wife, Margaret, had always said he was too hard on Nick. When they were married, she liked to point to an episode when Nick was eight years old and Robert, frustrated by years of swimming lessons in which Nick never actually entered the pool, threw Nick (with water wings) into the shallow end. Margaret felt guilty Nick was an only child.

As if to taunt Robert, the coffee shop was filled with successful-looking men in their early thirties—Nick's age—dressed in tailored suits, checking their phones. They took their coffee in lidded cups and left, no time to waste. Robert couldn't help thinking: my son could have been a lawyer, my son could have been a doctor, my son could have been anything he wanted to be. He had fantasies about Nick coming to his senses and asking Robert if he thought it was too late to attend graduate school. Robert always imagined himself taking the high road. He would not mention the trust fund that Nick had donated to an orphanage in India. Instead, he would write an enormous check, right there on the spot, no questions asked, no repayment necessary.

But Nick entered the coffee shop wearing a filthy bandana and jeans that were ripped at the knees—hundreds of thousands of dollars in private-school tuition down the drain. The people he sidled by looked over and around him, as if he were a blight on their morning view. He padded towards Robert's table in leather sandals with socks. He was not wearing deodorant.

"Hey, Pops. You look like you're dressed for a funeral." Nick plopped down sideways in the opposing chair. His face was beginning to slacken, his forehead creased in a permanent squint from the sun. Robert resented him for this: if your kid looked old, where did that leave you?

"Jesus, you've really let yourself go." The words came out before Robert could stop them.

"I'm real, Pops. All natural." Nick pinched the flesh of his leathery cheek. "These teeth, this hair, no artificial ingredients. All mine."

"I'm not asking you to get Botox." Robert lowered his voice when a man glanced up from his phone. "Just go to a dentist every once in a while. Don't spend so much time in the sun."

"To please whom? Should I worry about what others think of me, or be true to myself?"

"You're not wearing that to your mother's wedding, are you?" Robert found the lid to his coffee cup and jammed it on.

"I'm going dumpster diving later to see what I can find."

"Do you think that's appropriate?" Robert took a sip of coffee; Nick looked on with disdain.

"Actually, she rented a tux for me. I told her I'd wear it just this once, as a favor."

"Her new husband will be grateful."

"Dan? He's a mellow guy, actually. He doesn't mind."

"You've met him?"

"They came out to Kona. The guy can surf."

"A man of many talents." Robert had glimpsed Dan a couple of times at the Racquet Club. He always appeared to be going to or coming from the squash courts. It did not help that he was a successful hedge fund manager and was five years Robert's—and Margaret's—junior.

Things had gone downhill from there. Nick had refused a cup of coffee, feeling it necessary, once again, to explain to his father that he did not believe in currency or caffeine or society's constraints. Robert had told him that it was time to grow up. Nick had leapt up from his seat and pulled the sulky barista aside. The barista had gone back into the kitchen and come out with a bag of expired pastries. The entire coffee shop had learned of his and Nick's relation when Nick swung the bag overhead, shouting, "Over here, Pops! Score!"

On the phone, Nick's girlfriend had told Robert the address where Nick lived. She'd given Robert a list of belongings Nick needed at the hospital: underwear, socks, toothbrush, toothpaste, comb, Chapstick, and a change of clothes to wear home, instructing Robert to pick them up at Nick's place on the outskirts of town. Robert took a taxi there from the airport. It was a dumpy lime-green apartment building that doubled as a cheap motel. There were moldy shoes outside of doors, rag rugs hanging over peeling banister rails, and motorcycle parts like animal remains strewn over a patch of prickly lawn. A dumpster was turned on its side, beckoning rats. The area smelled of decay.

Robert knocked on the door with a MANAGER sign, thinking it was an office, but the manager, an overweight, thick-lipped man, appeared in a tank top and flip-flops, groggy even though it was afternoon. He did not try to hide the fact that he had just gotten out of bed; a rumpled, sweat-stained sheet trailed him to the door. Robert explained who he was. The manager rubbed his unshaven face and went in search of a key. When he returned, he held it just out of reach, as if expecting Robert to lunge for it. Then he deposited it in Robert's hand.

"Did he pay rent on time?" Robert asked.

"Didn't pay a dime."

Robert felt for his wallet inside his jacket. He'd brought blank checks just for this purpose. "How much did he owe you?"

"He didn't deal in money. We had an exchange."

Robert thought, Drugs, but the manager said, "He maintains the building. I've watched him snake a drain in under three minutes. He could be a plumber or an electrician if he put his mind to it."

"I don't think he's ever put his mind to anything. He isn't too much of a nuisance, I hope."

"Plays guitar, but always keeps it down. Spends a lot of time picking through the trash and making things on that there balcony." The manager rubbed his belly as if it were a child that needed reassurance. "I'm sorry about the accident." The manager shook his head.

"Yeah, well." Robert raised the key to signal his departure.

He found Nick's apartment at the end of the balcony, the last in a row of splintery brown doors. From the balcony, you could see the ocean, hear the waves crash along the rocky shore. The railing was covered in bird shit. A tenant in a tank top and flip-flops—the uniform of the unemployable—made his way to the parking lot, to a beat-up car. A cat rubbed against Robert's legs, wanting to be let in.

The apartment—if you could call it that—was a small room with a rust-stained sink. No toilet. Robert was expecting a mess—laundry, takeout cartons, a pyramid of beer cans—but the room was bare, with a thin twin mattress and a small wooden table with one drawer. There was a folded sheet and a stack of books at the foot of the mattress. The cat darted to a far corner, to a coconut shell filled with kibbles. A faint scent of patchouli hung in the air. Robert had thought he would have to ransack the room to find what he needed, but the clothes—Nick appeared to own only one pair—were tucked in a cubby. The toothpaste and toothbrush were laid out on the sink. He picked up a mesh bag made of old fishing net—clearly a dumpster find—and chucked Nick's belongings inside.

He wished Margaret were here; this was her area of expertise. But she'd twisted her ankle skiing with Dan, and besides, she was the one who, two months earlier, had posted Nick's bail when he'd been caught tampering with a logging truck. Since the divorce, five years earlier, they'd divvied up duties. She made a point not to overlap.

Margaret might have touched and smelled things, reminiscing about the time Nick swallowed a marble, how they'd celebrated with champagne when it finally came out, but Robert thought only of the task at hand. He opened the table drawer in search of Chapstick. It was the desk of someone who lived in a dreamworld: dried seaweed, paint brushes, a shell necklace, a plastic baggie of sand. No computer. No writing utensils. Nick had never understood that at some point in life you had to become useful, buckle down and get a job. When Robert found a paper clip in the back of the drawer, he felt like clapping.

Sure, he was sorry that Nick had been in an accident, but there was also—not that he would broadcast this—a sense of relief. He'd always known there would be some sort of retribution for Nick's way of life—he'd been waiting for it, actually—and now it had come. Robert had set money aside for this day the way other parents did for graduations or weddings. Nick didn't have any health insurance, of course.

As a kid, Nick was not only scared of swimming, but of bicycles, tunnels, dogs, public restrooms, sirens, and the dark. He had night terrors, and wouldn't eat unless he was sitting in Margaret's lap. If Margaret went to the bathroom, he clung to her feet. He had skin rashes and was allergic to tree nuts. He liked to stick small objects in his ears. He was a frequent visitor to the emergency room and had his tonsils and adenoids removed at the age of two. Robert and Margaret had wanted to have a second child, but Nick took everything out of them.

Robert had jabbed Nick with an EpiPen while dialing 911, watched Nick choke on his own vomit as he came out of anesthesia, and rescued a terrified, trembling Nick from the snarling jaws of a toy schnauzer. Robert barely recovered from one incident only to be blindsided by the next. Margaret lost herself in parenting support groups, learning how to deal with Nick's tantrums. She created charts with stars, and typed up step-by-step parenting instructions, which she posted around the house. On the bathroom mirror there'd been a sign that said: IN RESPONSE TO WHINING OR ANNOYING BEHAVIOR, TAKE A DEEP BREATH AND IGNORE. In the front hallway: WELCOME HOME TO YOUR CHILD! BE RESPECTFUL! USE A POSITIVE TONE OF VOICE!

It was relentless.

What you couldn't know, or understand, as the parent of a young kid, was that at some point the whole thing would become unsustainable. As a survival mechanism, you had to give up, let go. Nick had made this easy for Robert by choosing to live as a derelict.

So now that Nick had landed in the hospital, it was cause for concern, but Robert's heart didn't skip a beat and he didn't have to catch his breath. His hands were steady as he tied the handles of the fishing-net bag into a knot. And the fact that his son hadn't turned out the way he'd wanted him to was—in this case—a blessing. The impact was minimal. It could have been a former neighbor or a childhood friend.

Robert looked inside a bucket-turned-trash-can under the sink: empty. It was almost too easy. He was planning on calling Margaret to complain, but he couldn't find a reason.

He took out his phone anyway and dialed.

"Did you see where he lives?" he said when she picked up.

"Robert. I saw the apartment building but I didn't go in."

He could tell she was not in the mood to talk—she liked to wind down in the evenings, read her magazines—but he kept on anyway.

"It's depressing."

"It depends on how you look at it."

"It's the room of someone who sits around doing nothing all day."

"We don't know that for a fact."

"You think he secretly got a law degree without telling us?"

"No, but I think he's starting to come into his own. When Dan and I went out there a couple of months ago, he showed us a sculpture he built out of garbage. He's talented, Robert. We need to give him credit."

Margaret was forever defending Nick and his various preoccupations, which, according to Robert's calculations, had an average lifespan of three months. Robert didn't get it. What was there for a parent to be proud of? That Nick could perform a kind of massage that cleansed your organs? That he could live without money by bartering with shells? Whatever it was, Robert had heard it before, in all of its glorious versions. Nick was always flushed and breathless with new schemes, new ways to shirk responsibility, new strategies to avoid becoming an adult.

Margaret, for her part, seemed happy to go along for the ride, which involved no small amount of self-delusion. She would have let Nick wear diapers as a five-year-old if Robert hadn't stepped in. She allowed Nick to eat with his hands until college.

"Did he go surfing with Dan?" Robert asked.

"Yes. Why?"

"Never mind. I'll call you after I see him in the hospital." Robert snapped his phone shut.

Robert spotted a piece of paper stuck to the back of the apartment door. It was a note from the girlfriend. It was written in a slanted, childish script. She either didn't understand punctuation or couldn't be bothered to use it. He had to rip it off the door and hold it at an angle to decipher the crooked words. Her name was Char (short for Charlotte, Robert presumed). She wrote that she hadn't told him everything on the phone. She would meet him in the waiting room of the hospital that evening after she got off work.

Robert drove through the palm-speckled town, looking for a sign for the highway. The traffic was stalled; American tourists stopped their cars in the middle of the street to take in the ocean view. The pedestrians were worse, the way they hobbled along lugging their excess flesh like bags of sand. Some stood outside of an ice-cream shop, mauling vase-sized cones. It should have been a scene of care-free tranquility, of vacation—which Robert couldn't remember the last time he'd taken—but all he could see were the medical bills piling up. How many of these people would go into cardiac arrest tonight? Within the next six months? Why couldn't they ride an exercise bike the way Robert did every morning at dawn? At least Nick had that going for him: he wasn't overweight. He lived off of sunflower seeds and quinoa and seaweed, stuff Robert hadn't known was meant for human consumption.

The highway was bordered by black lava rock, the kind of land-scape you'd expect to find on the moon. People had configured small white stones to form words that could be seen by passing cars. But one dash of wind or rain turned it all to rubble, as evidenced by the myriad garbled rocks strewn about. For all Robert knew, Nick had been out here, spending hours piecing together futile messages about love and peace. If only he could put that energy towards building a career. Robert saw a sign for the hospital and turned off the highway.

The hospital smelled reassuringly of disinfectant. The two women who worked behind the information desk wore oversized flowered shirts and appeared as though they might break out into song. One, who exuded hibiscus perfume to match, pointed Robert down the hall to Nick's room. Her expression did not reveal anything about Nick's condition. Robert walked into Nick's room, bracing himself for a "Hi Pops!" but Nick was asleep.

Robert pulled up a chair and sat down next to the bed. Nick did not look good. His face was unnaturally swollen, a wad of gauze taped over one eye. His neck was in a brace. There were deep cracks in his lips. He had a blue tinge to his skin, as if he had hypothermia even though it was eighty-five degrees. The eye that wasn't bandaged was oozing pus. A nurse in a shirt depicting palm trees—you had to wonder how these people took themselves seriously—came in and told Robert that Nick had been sedated. She glanced at Nick and wrote something on a chart. When her beeper went off, she excused herself, saying she would let the doctor know Robert was here. Robert tried to remember if he had ever seen Nick look worse.

Two weeks out of college, Nick had ignored the pleas of Robert and Margaret and hopped on a plane to Bombay with the vague notion of helping people. When he returned six months later, he was riddled with worms and a skin disease that caused him to lose hair, leaving scaly patches of scalp. He couldn't sleep in beds anymore; he lay on the hardwood floor of Robert and Margaret's living room like a mangy dog.

After Nick was dewormed and his hair grew back (thinner and darker than it had been before), Robert landed him a trading job through one of his friends, but Nick hopped on another plane, this time to Ecuador.

From then on, it was all a blur. Nick was in Peru. Nick was in China. Nick was trekking in Nepal. Nick was on a boat somewhere, assisting a biologist studying the migration patterns of arctic terns. Nick was back in India, working for Mother Teresa then surfing in Goa. Nick was drinking goat blood with the Maasai in Kenya. Nick was building houses, then assembling wheelchairs, then making (and probably smoking) glass pipes in a country they'd never heard of. He crossed borders and mountain passes; they couldn't keep track. They received postcards. They followed his instructions, mailing letters to various hostels and poste restantes, never sure if the letters got there or if he ever bothered to read what they wrote.

Margaret went back to school to become a physical therapist. Robert doubled his list of clients, rarely made it home before ten. They told each other it was their way of relinquishing Nick and moving on.

On his twenty-fifth birthday, Nick sent home a picture of himself, twenty pounds thinner, with a long beard and bone studs in his ears. Margaret stared at the picture for days and cried. Robert cut it up and put it out with the trash.

The girlfriend, Char, was easy to pick out because she was the only one in the waiting room under the age of sixty. She appeared to be flipping through some kind of leather-bound day planner, ticking off things with a golf pencil. Robert had expected some sun-damaged floozy baring her midriff, like all of Nick's former girlfriends, but she was pale, her hair thick and black. She was wearing a long-sleeved shirt and a sundress over it that went down to the tops of her feet. Margaret had worn this type of dress when she was pregnant with Nick to hide her swollen ankles.

When Robert approached her, she stood up. "Do you want to walk?" She didn't wait for an answer, taking off down the hall in the direction of an unlit exit sign. Robert followed her past open doorways, glimpsing IVs and leftover trays of food. He expected to see at least one person crying, but everyone seemed content, eating jello or playing cards.

"How do you know you've got the right person?" he asked, when she pushed open a side exit door and stepped out into the sun.

She looked at him, laughed harshly. "Maybe any person will do. Actually, you two look alike."

"Don't tell Nick that."

"We call him Nico here."

They sat down on a bench that looked out onto a scruffy patch of crabgrass. If there was something else to see, Robert couldn't find it. Back East, there would be a statue of some sort, or at least an interesting tree, but here nobody could be bothered. Or they didn't want anything to compete with their shirts. Char crossed her legs and angled herself away from the sun. She shielded her eyes with a hospital pamphlet. Still not satisfied, she reached into her bag and pulled out a straw hat. Robert decided she was the most presentable out of any of Nick's girlfriends. Too bad she couldn't write a proper sentence.

"I know this thing is ridiculous," she said, batting the rim of her hat, "but it's the only one I could find that covers my whole face."

"I never thought I'd meet a girlfriend of Nick's who didn't worship the sun." This, for some reason, lifted Robert's spirits. He appreciated that she didn't feel the need to expose every inch of skin. She had potential.

"We've been seeing each other for almost two years."

Robert couldn't help himself. "Why him?"

"Well, first of all," she said, repositioning the hat, "I had severe acne when we first met. He was the only one who would give me the time of day."

"You'd never know."

"Nico's gifted," she said.

Robert stared at the crabgrass in front of them, refrained from commenting.

"I'm not sure how much he tells you, but he made a trash sculpture honoring a dead sea turtle that swallowed a plastic bag and it's generated a lot of buzz around the island. They've commissioned another one for the town hall and he just received a state grant."

Robert couldn't understand why people were forever championing Nick. It was as if they got swept up in his fantasy world, so much so that they became blind to the truth. Margaret—the blindest of them all—was always telling Robert to wait and see, as if Nick would someday be president.

Robert felt his mood plummet.

"What does he do for work?" Robert did not view this so much as a question, than as a way to steer Char towards the hard facts.

The girl just laughed.

"What do you do for work?"

"I'm a massage therapist."

She took Robert's hand and kneaded it. Robert tried to pull away, but she refused to let go, digging into his palm, snapping his fingers, telling him that she was a professional and he needed to relax. When she released him after a minute or two, he reached out for her, thinking he might fall off the bench. She politely offered up her forearm, as if swooning were a common side effect of her presence. Robert clasped on.

"I mean, we'd all like to be artists," Robert said. "I dabbled in improv myself in college."

"Dizzy?" she said. "Try to breathe."

"I even tried stand-up," he said, staring at the tattoo on her wrist. If he wasn't mistaken, it was a fetus. Nick's girlfriends were not known for their subtlety or good taste.

"Remember any good jokes?"

"I was booed off the stage." Robert tried to laugh, but found that he couldn't.

Patients were milling about now, doing feeble laps around the patch of grass. A woman—clearly a paid companion—picked a waxy leaf off the ground and waved it in front of a decrepit old man. The man could no more recognize the leaf than his own name. He was looking up at the sky, pointing a disfigured finger. Robert, knowing he could not count on Nick, had bought long-term-care insurance and set aside additional funds in an account for such a companion, who would delight and instruct long past the point there was any quantifiable benefit to the recipient.

The door behind them opened. A baby cried. Char covered her nose and mouth with her hand, saying the smell of the disinfectant in the hospital made her nauseous. Robert looked down at her ankles. They were not thin.

It all made sense to him now. He knew what she wanted to tell him: she was pregnant. But she and Nick—unlike Robert and Margaret at the time—were in no position to raise a child.

Robert let go of her forearm and steadied himself. "Let me guess. You need money for an abortion."

"God, no."

"You're planning on having the baby? What kind of life would that be? Do you think that Nick for one second understands responsibility? He's never been able to hold down a job."

"Do I look that fat?"

"It's the dress."

"I'm not pregnant." She stood up abruptly, fumbling with the straw hat.

The door behind them opened again and the nurse in the palm tree shirt called out Robert's name. The doctor would speak to him now.

The doctor, who was so young Robert decided he was a child prodigy, wasn't able to tell Robert much: the ribs would heal (they hadn't punctured an organ) but the eye was still questionable. They would operate to remove the damaged tissue. At least the doctor was wearing a plain white coat without floral motif. The two of them stood over Nick, who was still sedated, and the doctor waved his hands over Nick's body, pausing over bruises and cuts, pointing out stitches on his elbow and calf. The doctor considered Nick lucky; a man in a surfing accident a year earlier was still in a wheelchair. The doctor wasn't against surfing, but he couldn't understand why men—because it was always men—Nick's age (a lot older than the doctor) couldn't stay away from the coral, the rough conditions, or the rocks, as if they were magnetically drawn to risk. The doctor looked down at Nick, and Robert thought he saw him shake his head. Here was a young professional who understood the obligations and responsibilities of life well beyond his years. Still, Robert inspected the diplomas from Johns Hopkins and Oregon Health & Science University on the wall. They looked real. The doctor was telling him not to worry, there were options, always options. Worst-case scenario: a prosthetic eye. He was getting ready to ease Nick off the sedatives. As if they were in agreement on all things, including that the doctor was a winner and Nick a loser, they shook hands. The doctor said he would check back soon.

That night, Robert stayed at a business hotel near the airport. He called Margaret but she was already asleep and he was forced to talk to Dan. Dan described their skiing trip in Switzerland. He was one of those people who'd never learned how to summarize. Robert, who'd only been skiing twice (in New Hampshire, on two hellishly icy days), pretended room service was knocking on the door so he could get off the phone.

The following morning at the hospital, Nick was awake. He was sitting up in bed, telling the Palm Tree Nurse about the wave he caught that ultimately tumbled him into the rocks. He was telling it the way you would a triumph, no lesson learned. Robert wanted to add that a week later, here he was, hunched and shivering in a hospital gown. Nick shifted his buttocks and grimaced, baring a gray front tooth as egregious as a fang.

"Is that from the accident?" Somewhere along the way, Robert had stopped greeting Nick.

Nick tried to look down at his body, but his neck was immobile. "My ribs?"

"Your tooth."

Nick touched his mouth. "The front one? It's been that way for years, Pops. Surfboard whacked me in the face, remember?"

"I forgot."

"Anyway." He fingered the bandage that covered his right eye. "The good news is after the surgery I get to wear an eyepatch."

"How is that good news?"

"I've always wanted to be a pirate."

"I'm not sure you understand the gravity of the situation." Robert would have liked to slam down his fist, but there was no room on the flimsy tray table, which was covered in vacuum-sealed cups of applesauce.

"Just trying to look on the bright side, Pops."

Robert walked over to the window and put his palms against the glass. He didn't want to lose his temper. Margaret had accused him of using work to close himself off from the world. She said he'd lost the ability to process his emotions and be in a meaningful relationship with another human being. But it had never occurred to him—not even the remotest possibility—that she would leave.

"I met Char," Robert said.

"She's beautiful, huh?"

Outside, a patient dropped a roll of some sort and the birds went at it. Robert looked at his hand. "We had a nice conversation."

"Did she tell you she got into grad school?"

"No."

"The UPenn midwifery program."

"She didn't mention it."

"It means we're moving to Philadelphia."

"Away from the ocean?"

"And you'll like this part, Pops. She's going to make an office man of me. No more dumpster diving, at least for a while. I'm going to be working like a dog to pay the bills while she's in school."

Robert turned from the window. "Doing what?"

"I don't know, Pops. Something serious. You'll have to help me pick out a suit."

Char caught up to him at the vending area down the hall. The automatic coffee machine wasn't working, spewing coffee out before ejecting the cup. Robert was holding the empty cup, turning around and around, wondering where he should go to complain.

"Listen, what I was going to tell you yesterday?" She took the cup from him and handed it back full.

"I apologize about my mistake."

"Forget it."

She was dressed in a cotton skirt and sandals. This pleased Robert very much. If she were to come to the bank looking for him, say when school was out on break, say to grab a quick lunch, he wouldn't have to exit through the back door as he'd done before with Nick. He wouldn't have to tell his coworkers it was a community service project, working with street people. She was not an embarrassment, and he hoped that it wouldn't be long before Nick caught on.

"I'm trying to pull it together," she was saying. "I'm thirty-five years old and I want to do something with my life."

She was wearing small pearl earrings. Robert guessed it was a sign she wanted to be taken seriously. Nick was right: she was beautiful, just not in a straightforward way.

"Better late than never," Robert said, words he had hoped to someday say to Nick.

"It's just that…" Her eyes were tearing up.

"Change is hard."

"I'm ready."

"Do you need money?"

"I've saved more than enough."

"Then what?"

"Nico doesn't get it."

"Believe me, I know. I've been trying for years to spell it out for him. Maybe together we can get through." Robert wanted to put his hand on her shoulder, but they'd only just met. He'd have to wait until they were better acquainted.

"I need to give myself a fair chance."

"You're doing the right thing."

"He thinks he's coming with me, but he's not."

"He's not?" Robert thought he must have misheard.

"I'm leaving today. I need you to tell him goodbye for me." With that, she ran down the hall, dodging a janitor's cart, and turned the corner.

Robert ran after her, out the main entrance. There was someone waiting for her in a tan car, engine idling. He watched her get in and slam the door. The car drove off, leaving Robert helpless and blinking in the too-bright sun. After Margaret left him, he'd taken every precaution to make sure he'd never be in this position again, but here he was, five years later, once again the fool. He circled back inside and ducked into the nearest restroom. He pulled out his phone. It would be 10 p.m. on the East Coast but this was urgent.

Margaret picked up on the seventh ring.

"She's leaving him!" Robert said, pressing his mouth into the microphone.

"Do you know what time it is?"

"Nick's girlfriend!" He was breathing hard.

"Char?"

"How come he never told me about her before?"

Margaret took her time answering, most likely cinching the belt of her robe. "He thought you'd disapprove."

"She's not like the others." Robert tried not to let his voice break. "She's a real go-getter."

"You knew about her?"

Margaret exhaled. "I was sworn to secrecy."

"You lied to me."

"I kept my word to Nick."

"They call him Nico here."

"I know."

"I miss you, Margaret." There, he'd said it. How had he been so calm during the divorce?

"That doesn't sound like you, Robert. Listen, call me tomorrow after the operation. I'm a nervous wreck thinking about Nick's eye. I've taken three sleeping pills. I can barely stay awake."

The doctor caught Robert in the hall outside the hospital cafeteria and told him the operation had been a success. Robert lowered his head and pushed against the wall with both hands. The doctor cupped his palm on the back of Robert's neck, as if surreptitiously taking his pulse.

"It's good news, you understand."

Robert nodded.

But he was thinking about Char speeding away, wondering who the driver was, how she'd enlisted his help. Margaret had had Dan waiting in the wings. He'd come to her office with a bum knee. She said they hadn't touched until after the divorce, but Robert could never be sure.

"I think it would be better if he heard the news from you," the doctor said.

"Right," Robert said.

Nick was out cold when Robert went into the room. Robert had bought a silver heart balloon (it was either that or macadamia nuts) at the gift shop and asked the woman to inscribe it *Love, Char*: a sure sign he needed to get back to the office. Margaret had told him there were other things she needed besides food, water, and air. You'd have thought they lived in poverty.

He sat in the chair by Nick's bed. The swelling in Nick's face had subsided leaving it skeletal and bruised. There was a milky fluid running down the side of his cheek. The bandages were bloody. Robert felt sick. He went out to the main reception area and tried to pay for the hospital bill, but the woman behind the desk said a young lady had already taken care of it.

He went back into Nick's room and plopped down in the chair, where he was eye-level with Nick's gangly, calloused toes. Nick woke with a start.

"The eye?" Nick said.

"You won't get all of your vision back, but it can stay."

Nick let out a raspy hoot.

And now how was Robert supposed to explain to Nick that while his eye was intact, the rest of him was about to be shattered? All along Robert had imagined he would be the one to deliver the bad news, the blow that would send Nick reeling, make him understand the devastation of failure and pain of regret, but he'd always pictured himself elevated, as if standing halfway up a flight of stairs. Now, in the hospital room, he could feel his son's breath on his arm.

"About Char," Robert said. He didn't know where to begin.

There are things about my wife I'll never understand. She refuses to eat bananas in the morning and she doesn't like the sun. She'll hold a lit firecracker in her hand, but she will not go near the sea. I know now that you do not give an umbrella as a gift because the word for umbrella sounds like the one for separation. I tried to give Jade one a year after we were married. She looked at me in horror and threw her hands up in the air. "Do you know what this means?" she said. After that, I let her handle everything. All I did was teach English. When parents had questions about their children, Jade answered. I just stood there and smiled.

I used to be my wife's tutor. She had trouble pronouncing the *th* sound. Each week, we met on the campus of Cheng Kung University and sat at a marble table in the shade near the lake. Jade brought questions to class, scribbled in Chinese in her notebook. She would translate them into English and I would answer. In America, was being a flight attendant a good job? It was decent. Did most American women work? They did. Were they happy? I thought so. I tried not to think about the ones who had dated me. Afterwards, Jade would explain that in Taiwan, women did not have much say. In Taiwan, women wanted to be flight attendants. It was a hard job to get because you had to be pretty and pass many tests. You had to speak English. Jade was thinking about becoming one because she wanted to travel to different places and experience freedom.

She was very serious. She carried a miniature abacus key chain with seven different keys, one of which unlocked her diary, another her bike. She dusted the table with a tissue before we sat down. She came prepared with sharpened pencils and carefully selected one from her transparent pencil case at the beginning of each class. She frowned when she concentrated and shook her head when I said something she didn't understand. She was hard on herself. If she forgot a word that I had taught her, she would write it in the back of her notebook one hundred times. From what I understood, her parents were hard on her. Jade had eczema on her neck and arms, and her parents thought it made her ugly. In ninety-degree weather, they insisted she wear long sleeves and scarves.

Sometimes she would come to class so deep in thought that I would say something just to say something and it would come out all wrong. I might mention I had been served overcooked rice for breakfast, all watery, and she would inform me it was called *xifan* and it was supposed to be that way. Or I might point to blood on the ground and she would tell me it was betelnut juice that someone had spit out. She would say, "Oh, Michael," as if I were hopeless, but then she would laugh and I could see tears in her eyes. That's when I'd think about asking her out. But then I'd look at her hair. It was straight and even, never out of place. Even on windy days, it barely moved. It reached down to her shoulders, the ends neatly trimmed. I didn't think she'd be interested in someone like me.

One time, at the beginning of class, she squinted at her notebook and closed her eyes. I waited for her to ask me a question, but her lips were still and all I could hear was her breath. There were dark circles underneath her eyes. She stayed like that for a minute before I asked what was wrong. With her eyes still shut, she told me her parents wouldn't let her be a flight attendant. They said she'd seen too many Western movies. Now that she was thirty years old, they wanted her to settle down. They'd been arranging meetings with a matchmaker. In the last week alone, she'd met three different men.

The first one was old. He had a mole on his chin with a long hair sprouting out of it—a sign of wisdom—and at times this hair dangled into his teacup. He told Jade stories with morals, and gave her little wrapped candies, as if she were a six-year-old child. The second one smelled of alcohol and had a temper. Jade could tell by the acne pocks on his cheeks. When her parents weren't looking, he put his hand on her thigh. The third was the best looking, but he was from the country and very traditional. He didn't ask Jade any questions, but only talked about himself. He wouldn't do anything without consulting the fortuneteller at his local temple. If Jade married him, she would have to stay home and serve him and his parents like a traditional Chinese wife.

Jade put her face in her hands. "I don't know what I'm going to do."

I tried to cheer her up. I told her in America there was a dating show on television and no one ever made a match. I'd seen a show where a woman threw a pie. I told her people were screwing up constantly, breaking up all the time.

"Look at my family," I said. "Two out of three of us kids were accidents and my parents bring this up every time money is tight. My mother and father have left each other a total of about ten times."

Jade sank down in her seat and laid her cheek against the table.

"What I'm trying to get at," I said finally, "is that you can keep your independence by marrying a Western man."

"What Western man?" she said. "I don't know any Western man."

I thought about what I'd done with the thirty-four years of my life. In the States, I worked in a deli, spooning out potato salad and carving luncheon meats. It was supposed to be a summer job, but lasted seven years. I once got a ticket for pogoing along the side of a highway, and the story appeared in the local paper the following day. It wasn't until I saw an ad, "Teach in Asia," that I did anything useful. Here, I was an English teacher and people respected me. Here, I might walk down the street and have people shake my hand. Besides, I'd been tutoring Jade for about a year and we'd become friends. I thought about this and said, "Why don't you marry me?"

"Don't joke," Jade said. She placed a clump of hair over her eyes.

"I'm serious," I said.

Jade slowly lifted her head and picked up her pencil as if to take notes. She looked out over Cheng Kung Hu, a small manmade lake in the center of campus. It had a bridge leading out to a tiny island in the middle. The water was only a couple feet deep, dotted with half-submerged rocks. Two teenagers stood at the edge holding hands, and someone, maybe a parent, took a picture. "My parents are rich," Jade said. "They want me to get married. If we get married, they will give us money and buy us an apartment."

"See?" I said. "It's that simple."

Jade fingered the rim of her silk scarf. When a plane flew overhead, she did not look up. "If I can't be a flight attendant, then I want to open a small *buxiban*, a cram school, instead. You can be the American teacher and teach American customs."

I held out my hand and we shook. "It's a deal."

So then we got married in a church where the priest spoke both Chinese and English. We had a reception at the China Flower Hotel and Jade paraded around in different gowns, with her parents following close behind draping silk shawls over her shoulders, claiming she might catch cold. For our honeymoon, we drove down to Kenting and stayed at the Caesar Palace Hotel. We kept a polite distance between us and took turns changing in the bathroom. At night, we went to separate beds. During the day, we strolled along the beach and climbed over rocks. When we looked out over the water, we faced different ways.

The following week, we moved into a new apartment with shiny white floors, which Jade and I alternated mopping every other day. She opened a small *buxiban*, and I installed whiteboards in the classrooms and put two desks for Jade and me in the lobby downstairs. Outside the front door, I hung up a sign that said YES, WE SPEAK ENGLISH. I decorated the school with letters of the alphabet and a poster in which a cartoon mouse carried a comma to a sentence. Jade put ads in the newspaper and called her parents' friends. Within a couple of weeks, we had fifty students enrolled and I was teaching class.

During Dragon Boat Festival, we watched races in the heat and Jade held a perfumed tissue over her nose because of the stench from the polluted river. Over Chinese New Year, she handed out red envelopes filled with money to all of her nieces and nephews and whispered their names in my ear. On Tomb Sweeping Day, we visited the graves of her ancestors to clear the trash and cut the weeds. I watched her burn ghost money. Jade bought me food and mailed our letters. She took me to the dentist and extended my visa. She stamped documents with a chop, signing my name. Together, we joined a *biaohui*, a private loan association in which Jade invested our money every month.

At night, I told Jade about the States. I described the grass and the trees and how you could drive for hours without seeing another car.

I spoke of lemonade stands and swimming pools and backyards with gardens. Jade said when we went there she would eat a hamburger for her first meal. We decorated an imaginary American house that we dreamed one day we could buy.

One night, Jade turned off the light so we could go to sleep, but then turned it back on.

"Why didn't your family come to our wedding?" she asked. She was sitting up in her bed, tracing a stripe on her sheet. We'd been married for about a year.

"We're not very close," I answered. "My brothers are somewhere in California, probably surfing. If I know my parents, they're watching separate TVs."

Jade held her sheet in her hand and nodded. "Here you do everything for your family," she said. "You stick together no matter what."

She turned off the light, but instead of getting back under her covers, for the first time she came over to me. For a while we both lay there, awkward, but then Jade put her hand on my chest, touching me here and there. She asked, "Does this feel good?" and moved on to other parts of my body. I followed along, doing the same. Then we forgot ourselves, and it was nice like that.

Afterwards, I listened to Jade mumble in her sleep, and when she rolled over, I could feel her breath against my arm. She brushed my shoulder and a warmth spread throughout my body. The next day was the day I gave her the umbrella. First, I went to a Chinese shop but the salesclerk shouted questions I couldn't understand. "*Gao,*" he kept saying to me. Tall. "I know, I know," I answered. He came over and reached his hand to the top of my head. At another store, the manager looked up at me in wonder and scratched his scalp. At a third, the whole staff, about five people, hid behind a door and stared. Finally, one of them came forward and handed me a note that said, "How tall are you?" I answered, "Six-one," and the staff broke out into hysterics. So I went to the one tourist shop in town. There, I looked at some wall hangings, but I couldn't read the characters. I looked at some clothes, but I didn't know my wife's size. I was about to leave the store when an English-speaking salesclerk with a thin mustache and a Mickey Mouse tie led me upstairs to a room filled with painted umbrellas. "What woman," he said, "can resist?"

When I held out the umbrella to Jade, she was in our room, slipping her arm through the sleeve of a cardigan sweater. She recoiled, as if I had presented her with a reptile instead. Her face immediately flushed a deep red.

"But the salesclerk told me..." I started.

She shook her head. "He thinks you have an American wife."

She explained to me then, holding one hand limp in the other, that because I had given her an umbrella, a rift would come between us. She did not know if this rift would be big or small.

"That sounds like an old wives' tale," I said, laughing out loud to make light of the situation.

Jade did not smile. "Let's hope so."

Then she turned her back to me to button her sweater, the way one was supposed to do, I imagined, in the kind of marriage we had made.

A week later, Mr. Lee first appeared outside my class. The upper half of the classroom door had a window through which parents could look to check on their kids. Mr. Lee knocked his glasses against this window and all of my students turned to watch, twisting in their miniature plastic chairs. I was teaching my youngest class, a group of six-year-olds. Mr. Lee's son, Ernie, was trying out the class. He was only five but he had just come back from a year in the States where he went to nursery school and got an English name. Mr. Lee held up a hand in apology. You might picture him fumbling with his glasses or smiling stupidly, forehead pressed against glass. But Mr. Lee rested one arm on the door as if observing a class was an everyday affair. He wasn't like the other parents who waved like they were standing on a cruise ship leaving shore. He watched Ernie and then focused his gaze on me, sometimes frowning, sometimes nodding. I was wearing purple shorts and a Donald Duck T-shirt, jumping around the room to get my students' attention. I started sweating. I felt like a fool.

After class, downstairs, I heard my wife talk to Mr. Lee. They discussed Ernie and the class. Mr. Lee loved the school, and by the way he listened to Jade, I could tell he was impressed she was the owner. He smiled at the alphabet on the wall, and when he saw the Statue of Liberty pen on my wife's desk, he practically shouted, clapping his hands. He complimented Jade, and Jade swatted the air, saying she didn't deserve the praise. Then, although my Chinese was pretty bad, I heard Mr. Lee say, "The foreigner is a good teacher." He said some other things I didn't understand. I waited for my wife to look over and smile. I waited for my wife to tell him I was her husband. My wife casually rearranged some things on her desk, pushing the phone over to the side so Mr. Lee could fill out an application for Ernie. She opened a drawer and took out a pen, saying, "The foreigner? He's not bad."

I watched Jade look at Mr. Lee when he talked. He gestured with his hands, and when he laughed, he took a step back and ran his fingers through his hair. They laughed together. My wife stood up and I almost expected her to hold on to Mr. Lee's arm to steady herself. After a while, she looked over. I was sitting at my desk, pretending to plan a class. She seemed to look through me at the wall behind my back. She brushed the hair out of her eyes. I smiled but she didn't see.

That night, I met my friend Josh at a bar where we drank Taiwanese beer and watched MTV. Josh taught English to one- and two-year-olds and had two assistants in each class to change diapers. His students were known as the "English babies" because when they grew up, they could speak English without an accent. The difference between Josh and me was this: The nights I went out, I came home at around twelve or one. Josh stayed out until seven the next morning. At seven, he usually went to McDonald's and passed out with his face in his tray. The weekend before, he was woken up by one of his student's parents.

I told Josh everything. I told him about Mr. Lee and how my wife laughed. I told him Jade had been walking around in a trance all day.

Josh took a sip of beer and wiped his mouth with his forearm. "That's bad news, dude," he said.

He ordered another beer and held the bottle up in a toast. "There's always another country," he said. "So you fuck up in the US and Taiwan. Try Spain."

When I got home, Jade was reading the newspaper in bed, still awake. We had moved the beds together, but there was still an inch-wide crack between them. I changed my clothes and climbed under my covers.

"I would like a back porch on that house," I said, rolling onto my side to face her.

"Would you believe Mr. Lee is a widower?" she said, as if talking about an article she had just read. "I don't know how he raises Ernie, takes care of his mother, and earns a living all on his own."

"Some of those big rocking chairs would be nice," I said.

"He makes the time to wake up every morning and do tai chi. Every Sunday, he and Ernie drive to Kaohsiung to practice the *pipa*."

"What the hell is a *pipa*?" I said.

My wife did not appreciate my tone of voice. She went back to reading the paper, saying, "It's too hard to explain."

During the next couple of days, I heard more about Mr. Lee. He wrote calligraphy and knew a hundred poems from the Tang Dynasty by heart. He was even a poet himself. "He's probably a painter too," I said to my wife. Jade did not appreciate my sarcasm either. "As a matter of fact he is," she said. "He goes to Alishan to paint. He has an exhibit called 'Clouds' at the Xin Lang Art Gallery."

That night, I asked my wife, "Do you want out?"

She was lying in bed, her hair fanned out on the pillow beneath her, staring into space. "I don't understand," she said.

"I mean do you regret getting married?" I said.

My wife looked at me as if I'd told her to jump off a cliff.

"I mean, you're still my wife, right?" I put my hand on top of hers.

Jade put her other hand on top of mine and looked at me sadly. She rubbed her hand back and forth across mine. "Of course I'm your wife," she said quietly. "What a silly question."

Ernie was by far the most advanced student in my class. He sat nicely in his chair and wasn't interested in showing anyone his underpants. "How's the weather?" I asked my class. That was usually the first question of the day. My students looked out the window and said, "It's raining." Ernie had a puzzled expression on his face.

He raised his hand and said, "I'd say that's more of a drizzle than a rain." I showed my class pictures of cats and dogs, and took out a flashcard of a big, green rabbit. "Rabbit," I said, "rabbit. Repeat the word after me." Ernie raised his hand and said, "That looks more like Tyrannosaurus rex." My students looked at Ernie, their mouths gaped open, and one girl said, "I don't understand." The littlest boy in my class began to cry.

After class, I told my wife, "This can't go on."

"There's nothing we can do," she said. "Ernie's too young to be in a higher class. He can't write."

I gave her the classroom report: a couple of red and blue markers had gone dry, and one of the kids had scribbled on the back wall. I volunteered to repaint it.

"Does Mr. Lee even know I'm your husband?" I said, as if this were just another item on the list I needed to check off.

Jade squinted, as if I'd pointed to something small across the room and asked her to identify it. "Of course he does. Of course he knows."

I started having dreams. Mr. Lee was in my class and he asked me questions about the subjunctive mood. I drew a game of hangman on the whiteboard to buy time. He corrected my English. I was so nervous, I made more mistakes. I said libary instead of library. Ernie asked me to explain the difference between a rabbit and a hare. The class laughed. Ernie crossed his arms over his little chest and said, "You mean you don't know?" Or, I was playing mahjong, and Ernie, Mr. Lee, and my wife were shuffling the tiles fast. Before I knew it, it was my turn, and the three of them were staring at me, impatient. They all started chanting something I couldn't understand, banging their fists on the table. Finally, Jade rolled her eyes and said, "We're waiting for you to discard."

"She's on a runaway train," Josh said when I saw him the following week, "and you can't catch it." He took a swig of beer, swished it around in his mouth, and swallowed.

Next thing I knew, Mr. Lee was bringing my wife presents. During Mid-Autumn Festival, he brought her moon cakes in a red box. When he came back from Taichung, he brought her sun cakes. He brought her peanut candy from Tainan County and chicken feet from Chinatown. He brought the things my wife loved. He gave her a shiny knot of string about the size of a football. Jade saw the expression on my face. "How can you not like Chinese macramé," she said. "It's beautiful."

On Teacher's Day, Mr. Lee invited us to dinner. Jade was sitting downstairs at her desk, checking attendance, and I saw her face turn red. "Really," she said, "you don't have to." She was being polite. Mr. Lee said a couple of things, and I could tell by the way he straightened his back and lifted his chin that he was probably talking about how it was his duty and honor. To my wife's dismay, I interrupted. I was tired of sitting at my desk like a wallflower at the other end of the lobby. I knew I was being rude, but I couldn't help myself. "What the hell?" I said, standing up from my chair. "Why don't we just go?"

And what a surprise! Mr. Lee could cook too. He brought out pickled cabbage, tofu and mushrooms, shredded pork, sweet-and-sour soup, stir-fried vegetables, meat stew, bamboo shoots, and braised duck. He apologized for serving so little food. "This is wonderful," Jade said, complimenting him on every single dish. "We don't eat like this very often," she said, and I prayed to God she wouldn't bring up my specialty, the Cheetos sandwich. She loved Mr. Lee's food, his house, and his calligraphy hanging on the walls. She nodded approvingly at the way Mr. Lee helped his mother get settled in her seat and patted her dry, wrinkled hand every time she looked around. Jade smiled when Mr. Lee put food in Ernie's bowl with his long, wooden chopsticks.

"How's school going?" Jade asked, smiling at Ernie and speaking English on my behalf. Ernie made fish lips and blew a bubble out of saliva. "You're too smart for your own good!" Mr. Lee said, pinching Ernie's nose. "Too smart!" Mr. Lee pretended to take Ernie's nose off and hold it in his hand. Ernie shrieked and climbed into Mr. Lee's lap. Jade laughed and Mr. Lee's mother smiled and clicked her tongue. Mr. Lee continued eating, sometimes feeding himself, and sometimes feeding Ernie, who sat perched in his lap with his mouth open like a baby bird.

I got up to go to the bathroom, and Mr. Lee pointed me through a sitting area filled with wooden carvings of elves standing on tree stumps and next to them boxes of toy dinosaurs. I had to duck underneath a paper pterodactyl hanging off a chandelier. In the bathroom, there was a small, plastic toilet set up next to the large, porcelain one. There was even a small, purple towel hanging below the large bath towels on the wall. I half-expected to find a miniature doorway as well.

When I came back, Ernie was sitting in Jade's lap and Mr. Lee and his mother were sitting on either side. Their heads leaned in toward Jade as if they were both discreetly smelling her hair. A flash went off, and I saw the camera on the table, propped up on a pile of folded dishtowels.

Mr. Lee turned to my wife and said, "*Ju li rong*," something I had heard before, but I couldn't remember what it meant. Jade bowed her head and pursed her lips as if he had paid her the highest compliment of all.

I sat down in my seat across from everyone and waited for them to slide their chairs back, but they continued to sit there, squeezed together, as if they were watching a television with a very small screen. I waited until I couldn't stand it anymore.

"So, what does '*ju li rong*' mean?" I said at last, trying not to botch up the pronunciation too bad. I crossed my arms over my chest to let them know I knew something was going on.

Jade looked around the room as if she felt a cool draft, but couldn't tell from where it came. Finally, she rested her eyes on me.

"That," she said, getting up and coming over to my side, "is my Chinese name."

During the next couple of weeks, I planned a Halloween party at the school with bobbing for apples, pin the tongue on the goblin, and a haunted bathroom. I kept myself busy decorating the school with cutout pumpkins and glow-in-the-dark skeletons. For the party, Josh volunteered to walk around dressed as a mummy and even Jade gave a half-smile at the idea of me being the dead man in the bathtub. I tried to show her how I was going to shout "Boo!" or maybe snore to scare the students, but she was busy talking to parents on the phone. I taught her how to say "Trick or treat," but she repeated the words as if it were a phrase you used when you didn't want to continue playing a long, boring game. "I'm getting tired of these holidays," she said.

On July Fourth, all of the students had decorated pictures of the American flag, and there was still glitter sticking to the floors and walls of the school. On Labor Day, a student had sprained his wrist falling down the stairs.

The evening of the party, Josh and I stood downstairs in the school kitchen, getting ready. Upstairs, there were children laughing, and I heard Jade say, "You got it!" I imagined a wet-haired student with an apple in his mouth. "Look at what we're reduced to," Josh said, opening a beer and taking a sip. He had gray streamers wrapped around his body from the neck down, and he was waiting for me to wrap up his head. I was dressed in black and wore a blond wig. Josh took a tube of fake blood and smeared it on my face and neck. He squeezed a glob onto the wig. "I need a beer for this," I said. Josh tossed one in the air and I caught it behind my back.

I lay waiting in the empty bathtub while Josh went upstairs to get a small group of students. I stretched out in the tub. For the first group, I decided I'd lie with one leg dangling over the side. Josh came in with three students and shined his flashlight on me. The kids stared for a while and one of them pinched my leg to see if it was real. I waited until they got relaxed and one of them started pulling the hairs on my arm. "Blah!" I shouted. The kids screamed and ran out of the bathroom.

"Not bad," Josh said. He went out and returned with a couple of beers. We relaxed for a few minutes until Josh went up to get the next group.

It took Josh five minutes to coax the next group to take a step into the bathroom. They all peered at me from the hallway, but didn't want to come in. By then, my wig was on crooked and I figured I looked like I'd been scalped. I wiggled my foot and the kids ran away.

This continued for a couple of hours, with Josh bringing me beers, keeping me supplied. Once, I was taking a sip of beer when he brought in a group of children, so I had to pretend to be dead with a beer can in my hand. "A dead drunkard," Josh said when he shined the light on me. "See? Alcohol is bad." The students nodded their heads and left.

When Josh led the last group down the stairs, I heard Ernie cry, "Oh my God," all the way from the third floor, probably pointing to the paper skeleton dangling from the ceiling. His voice sounded like the whine of a cat. Josh led the students in and pointed the flashlight at me. "It's not real," Ernie shouted. "My dad says it's not real. The blood is ketchup from McDonald's." He pointed to the cobweb, the bone in the sink, everything I had made, saying, "Not real, not real." I listened calmly until Ernie pointed at my face. Then I jumped up and grabbed him yelling "Ha!" The other kids screamed and ran away and I heard Josh calming one who was still yelling in the hallway. I held on to Ernie's little arms and pinned him down in the tub. He was dressed as a bumblebee and his yellow tissue-paper wings crumpled underneath him. The fake blood from my wig dripped down onto his yellow and black striped shirt.

"Ernie," I said, squeezing him by the shoulders. I figured I'd scare him so he and Mr. Lee never came back to this school. I made things simple and I spoke in the present tense. "I kill you," I said. This did not appear to be in Ernie's vocabulary, so I tried signals. I made a gun with my thumb and forefinger and put it to my head and slashed my hand across my throat. Ernie pulled my wig over my eyes and crawled out of the tub. I tried to jump out after him but I hit my forehead on the shower curtain rod. I fell and the shower curtain came tumbling down on top of me.

"Just look at you," my wife said, standing in the doorway with her arms folded across her chest. Ernie jumped up from the floor and ran out, saying, "Bye, Michael!" I knew my wife was angry because she could barely speak English. She stuttered and something came out in Chinese. She was shaking and it took her a while to think of the words. "Can't you do anything right?" she said. She picked up a beer can from under the sink and threw it at me. "Where did you go, Ernie?" she called, slamming the door on her way out.

That evening, Jade did not come home. I walked around the apartment, picking things up and putting them down. I noticed for the first time there was a row of tiny cactuses on the windowsill. I went into the living room to read and then got up to go to the kitchen, where I stood opening and closing the refrigerator door. The cool air felt good against my face. I took out an ice cube and chewed on it.

The linoleum floor was checkered with white squares and I counted thirty-six in all. I compared the clocks in the bedroom and the kitchen to make sure they said the same time.

When I got into bed, I couldn't sleep. I went out to the living room and turned on the TV and got back into bed. "*Bao qian*," someone was saying. Sorry. I heard the sound of someone else crying, then two people crying, then silence, no crying at all. Someone else came on and started singing a song.

Jade came home past two. I heard her pass through the living room. She turned off the TV and went into the kitchen where it sounded like she was pouring herself a drink. She breathed out heavily and slammed something against the counter. She paced back and forth for a while and her footsteps echoed as if she were walking through an empty house.

"Is everything okay?" I yelled from the bedroom.

"What does it matter?" Jade said, appearing in the doorway. Her hair stuck to her forehead like she'd been running in the rain. "Okay or not," she said, "I still have to live here." With her hand, she motioned around to show the apartment but the whole time she was looking at me.

"In the States..." I started to say.

Jade leaned with her back against the doorway, pulling her coat around her. "You have a good imagination," she said.

I grabbed my jean jacket and walked out the door. I walked down Dongmen Street and turned onto Shengli Road. I passed men chewing betelnut and playing pachinko, and hairless dogs fighting over garbage. I went by an old woman chasing a rat with a broom. I looked in on Josh, sitting alone, drinking in the bar. He was examining the front of his shirt as if he'd just spilled on himself. I was deciding whether or not I'd join him when an old man in front of a steaming cart whistled and waved at me.

This happened all the time. A man a foot shorter than me would ask to try on my jacket. Or a teenager would ask to put his foot in my shoe. People wanted to compare the size of their hands against mine. Children would shout "*juren*," giant, and dart to the side of the street. Old people stared.

But this old man could have been blind.

"*Baozi*," he said, gesturing to the meat buns he was selling. He motioned for me to come closer in and smell them. I did.

"*Baozi*," I said, pointing to the buns, and the man nodded his head and laughed.

I held up five fingers and the man said, "*Wu ge.*"

I nodded my head. "*Wu ge.*"

The man carefully picked up five meat buns with pincers and dropped them into a bag. He folded the top of the bag over so the buns would stay warm. I gave him some money and he counted out the change. He held the bag up to me with both hands and I carried it home like a trophy.

It was dawn when I got back to the apartment. Jade was sitting at her desk, cradling a cup of tea. She had one leg crossed over the other.

"*Baozi*," I said, placing the bag on Jade's desk.

Jade blinked for a moment, looking at the bag.

"*Baozi*," she said.

I opened the bag and took out the buns. I went into the kitchen and came back with napkins.

"You must eat," I said, putting a bun in front of her.

"That's okay," she said.

"But I insist," I said. "You must be hungry."

"You should keep them for yourself."

"I want you to have them," I said. "I got them for you."

Jade blew on her tea and took a sip, stretching her legs out underneath her desk. She folded some papers and stuck them in a drawer, pushing some bills to the back. She looked down, but when she turned her head to take a bite of the bun, the corners of her lips curled up the slightest bit. I waited, patiently, for her to look at me.

SILENCE

On an afternoon when Catherine was able to duck away from the Quiet Adventures tour group, in between two lectures she was signing for the traveling hearing-impaired, she took a taxi to a village outside of Taipei, to a small English school where she'd once taught. She'd lived on the third floor in a room with a bare bulb, an electric kettle, and a mosquito coil. There was a hole underneath a loose floor tile, the kind of place you could stash your valuables and return to find them twenty, thirty years later untouched. This was back during a brief hiatus from college, after the doctors informed her she was going deaf.

But the taxi pulled up to a luxury boutique hotel, the school building long gone. There was a manmade waterfall at the entrance, and a long semicircular pond resembling a moat with three large, radioactive-orange carp. She had to cross a cobbled footbridge to reach the door. Once inside, she was greeted by a line of staff who, in blue vests, resembled cheerful, well-groomed train conductors. It was a flashy hotel, full of etched glass and angled lights. Corners were softened with feathery tropical plants; the air smelled of nectar. Catherine heard a whirring sound that she at first mistook for her tinnitus before she looked up to see the ornate wooden paddles of a ceiling fan.

There was a burst of music, something harsh and jarring, without words, a song that could have passed for a car crash. She settled into one of the modern foam lobby chairs—comfort apparently out of style—and inserted an earplug. The world around her became muffled and indistinct. It was then that she saw something—the only thing—she recognized: the old marble drinking fountain. But there were no kids lined up, pushing each other's faces into the water. It was cordoned off like a quaint oddity now, an antique of which no one knew its function. The school had had two classrooms on the second floor and a small kitchen down below. Bare bones. Nothing like the mirage of smoke and mirrors she was sitting in now.

She was forty-eight. Against the advice of everyone she knew, she'd taken a leave of absence from her job as a speech therapist to volunteer abroad, float around Asia alongside half the world's population of aimless twenty-three-year-olds. The term "midlife crisis" had cropped up among her friends and family to help explain her erratic behavior, which began when both of her children went off to college and she asked her husband of twenty-five years for a divorce. But Catherine saw it more as a need to take a break from the superficialities—the tablespoon of flaxseed meal on her cereal each morning, the all-too-frequent trips to the car wash and the hygienist, the discussions about whether the kids should be allowed to have credit cards or, for the older one, a motorcycle—each day a carbon copy of the one before.

The last time she'd been here, she was a girl too young to know any better.

She read the lips of the concierge: he wanted to know if he could be of help. She told him she was meeting someone, a guest. She was early; she would wait. He bent in to listen, which meant her voice was too low.

Outside, a tour bus pulled up and a line of people stepped off with cameras like medallions dangling from their necks. Brides in gauzy finery posed for pictures, standing, sitting, kneeling, with bouquets and without. Children ran around with flower chains in their hair. Apparently the hotel was a popular destination for weddings.

The concierge nodded and backed off. She knew she would be taken at her word because she was a foreigner.

She'd come to Asia the summer after junior year in college, after her body unexpectedly failed her, to see (and hear) the world while she could. In her case, it was a great pressure on one side of her head, a heaviness that threatened to topple her over, draw her ear like a magnet to the ground. She lost all hearing on her right side; the doctors gave her prednisone, predicted another four, five months until it progressed to her left. So she bought a plane ticket to Kathmandu, granting herself the rest of summer and fall to live life before the silence arrived.

It was hard to believe she was going deaf; at that age, the worst thing she'd experienced was breaking up with boys. (She tried to explain it wasn't their fault. She was immature; she tended to lose interest.) But it was a good excuse to take a semester off from a small liberal arts college where she had developed a crush on her boyfriend's roommate. She trekked in Nepal for a week before getting robbed by a British couple, drunks. She knew if she phoned her parents, they would beg her to call it good, come home, put the pictures she'd taken in a fine leather album to show her future children. They would give her the latest news on a handsome neighbor she'd once kissed—Bobby Anderson—who was about to graduate from law school at the top of his class, the implication being she should rush home and snap him up in the little time she had left.

Instead, she went to Taipei because she'd heard Americans could make quick money teaching English. For two weeks, she stayed at an overcrowded youth hostel, where the only way to have privacy was to loop a towel through a slat from the bunk above and pull it down like a shade. The first night, a Danish woman instructed her to sleep clutching her money belt to her chest. In the mornings, she woke up with cramped fingers that would not straighten until afternoon.

Everyone in the hostel was looking for work, looking for a way to get out, to find a place where they might have a proper bed or a room with a door. Taipei was a mob scene; any time she waited in line for a bus, she got trampled once it arrived. Cars and motorbikes clogged the streets, an endless, stalled parade. Because the Foreign Affairs Police had been cracking down, jobs for foreigners were scarce. She was turned down at four schools, where they told her they were hiring only English-speaking Chinese until the police stopped their raids.

Then, a stroke of luck. Walking a rented bicycle through a street market, a man approached her. He had nice eyebrows, thin, quivery lips, the unlined forehead of someone her age. "My English is very poor," he said, hoarsely, handing her a square of paper:

THE BEST ENGLISH SCHOOL IN THE WORLD IS LOCATED IN A SMALL VILLAGE OUTSIDE OF TAIPEI WHERE THE HOT SPRINGS CAN BOIL EGGS AND THE CRICKETS OUTNUMBER THE CARS. IF YOU AGREE TO TEACH ENGLISH CONVERSATION, I WILL PAY

YOU AND PROVIDE ROOM AND BOARD. MY SISTER, MEIMEI, WILL COME MOST WEEKENDS TO PREPARE DELICIOUS FOOD. YOU HAVE TWO MINUTES TO DECIDE.

Before Catherine could finish reading, the man passed her an envelope, which, she was embarrassed to discover, contained a hundred-dollar bill. No one else seemed to notice: the street sellers went about their business, shaking tea in canisters and steaming buns. Catherine's taking the envelope in her hands—it would have dropped to the ground, otherwise—seemed to seal the deal.

Mr. Wang—that was his name—escorted her back to the hostel on his motorbike, and told her he would come in his car to pick her up the following day.

"He wants something from you," the girls in her dorm room said. "You don't get money for nothing here." They sat on a cot playing cards and blowing smoke rings, and didn't invite her to join them. That night she lay awake, thinking: a brothel? No. The man was clean-shaven, soft-spoken. He wore a light blue polo shirt buttoned up to his neck. She could tell by his lopsided smile that it had been hard for him to approach her. And she with her baseball cap and ponytail was hardly the prostitute type.

He came as promised in a small, cream-colored car. She had one bag, a green knapsack, which he ceremoniously hoisted into the trunk. During the forty-minute drive, for most of which they were stuck in traffic, he reached into the backseat (which was too small for passengers) and offered up bags of peanut candy and seaweed crackers, enough food to last a week. He chewed noisily in place of conversation. They left the city, passing large warehouses and rice fields, until they reached a village that was just an intersection. He pointed out the noodle stall and the small market displaying oscillating fans and fly swatters in pastel colors. There was no traffic light.

"You won't get lost," he said, his voice catching.

"Yes, I think I'll be able to find my way around."

It was unmistakably a school, she was relieved to see, brand new, chalky white, with stately-looking columns bracketing the entrance.

There was a Z-shaped wheelchair ramp that emptied out by a swing. She could already envision the mad rush: students bursting out the door and jumping the rails, vying to be the first to hop in the canvas seat.

"All yours?" she asked, because she owned only the contents of her knapsack. And she wondered how he—not exactly the go-getter type—could have so much more.

His parents had given him the money, he admitted sheepishly. The car was theirs too.

"My parents won't give me anything until I get married," she said.

He lowered his head, as if to duck her comment.

The walls inside the school were rough and unpainted. There were metal chairs stacked by the door, unopened boxes of cleaning and classroom supplies. He would spend the week setting up and preparing for the school to open the following Monday. He hoped he would get it done in time.

She'd painted for two summers in college; she was happy to help.

He almost flinched at her offer. And so that was what he had wanted.

The following morning, she awoke to the smell of hot soybean milk and fried dough sticks from the market. He had set breakfast out for both of them downstairs in the foyer on a cardboard box turned upside down. It didn't matter if she sat with her good ear to him: the place was so quiet, his voice—hoarse as it was—seemed to surround her.

"What kind of name is Catherine?" He had only the faintest hint of an accent, the lilt of his intonation a fraction too slow.

"I don't know. A long one. My friends call me Cat."

"An animal's name?"

She explained it was short for Catherine.

"Surname?"

"Davis."

"Are you engaged to be married?"

"No. What's with all the questions?"

"I want to learn everything." He coughed into the back of his hand.

They scraped and sanded and painted until evening—no lunch— at which point he more than made up for the skipped meal with

Styrofoam containers of noodles and dumplings and fried rice and clear soup. Sometimes, he leaned back and ate with his eyes closed. Other times he hovered over his soup, so close she could see his eyebrows reflected in the broth.

"Is your tatami comfortable, Miss Davis?" He pointed overhead, referring to the mat she slept on two floors above. His voice surprised her, sounding like it was teetering on the edge of something, about to fall off. He was sleeping in the kitchen, she noticed, on a tatami identical to hers. He rolled it up during the day and stuffed it behind the fridge.

"It's fine."

"Much harder than a mattress."

"Where did you learn to speak English so well?"

He flushed. "I have trouble with my pronunciation."

"You speak perfectly."

"I have good days and bad."

With that, he was silent for the rest of the meal. He cleared his throat when he got up from the table, tipped an invisible hat to wish her a good night.

The next day, he scared her by stepping out from the second-floor bathroom, where he'd been installing a paper-towel dispenser, to thrust a piece of paper in her hand. She fumbled, almost dropped it, said, "What's this?" He didn't answer, stared at the paint-flecked knuckles of her hands until she unfolded it and read: FROM NOW ON, I WILL COMMUNICATE WITH YOU ONLY IN WRITING. IF YOU FIND AN ERROR, PLEASE CORRECT AND RETURN IT TO ME.

"You've got to be kidding," she said.

TO PRACTICE MY SPELLING. He wrote in his notepad, nodding grimly, as if the burden were all his.

"You don't understand." She exhaled audibly. "I might be reading notes for the rest of my life." But even saying it out loud didn't make her believe it.

He offered to pay her additional for her trouble, but she shook her head vaguely, internally scolding herself for not taking the money, which—if she saved enough—would allow her to fly back to Nepal and pick up where she'd left off. She convinced herself he would grow tired of writing, that it was a passing phase.

In the days that followed, he'd come to her unannounced, once or twice a day, standing quietly in her vicinity, a square of paper in hand, until she looked up. She learned to detect his presence in the stillness, to feel the vibrations of his padding feet, to sense his arrival like dawn. He had a habit of pausing outside of doorways, as though to catch his breath. Sometimes he didn't appear, instead leaving his notes folded up on the overturned box by the breakfast he'd set out or pinned to the bulletin board he'd nailed to the wall in the hallway. On those occasions, she found herself carrying the note upstairs to her room and opening it in secret like a schoolgirl.

At first, he wrote necessary information: the Spackle was located in the kitchen drawer, the heavy-duty primer under a tarp out back. If the fumes got to her, he had a variety of masks. He let her know by early afternoon what they would be eating for dinner.

Then, a question: DO YOU PREFER THE COLOR OLIVE OR BEECH? He'd been staring at the entryway to the school—the last section to be painted—and wanted her opinion on what was, apparently, a momentous decision in his life. To humor him, she gazed at the paint cans he labeled in English for her, the sample swatches he taped to the wall. In the end, she chose beech after lying awake and thinking about it all night. They worked on the front hall together, meticulously—beech it was—spent practically the same amount of time it had taken them to paint the rest of the school.

There were observations: THIS MORNING I WOKE UP TO JUBILANT CLOUDS PARADING ACROSS THE HEAVENS LIKE PEACOCKS. THE JET PLANE THAT TORE UP THE SKY (WITH JEALOUSY?) WAS NO MATCH.

He related obscure facts: DID YOU KNOW BY COUNTING THE TIMES A CRICKET CHIRPS IT IS POSSIBLE TO TELL THE TEMPERATURE OUTSIDE?

The notes looked like formal invitations, painstakingly printed in all capitals, the letters spaced far enough apart that they stood alone at the same time they formed words. He never made a mistake, not once. They came on crisp squares of rice paper, which she inevitably touched with her tongue and held up to the light. He signed each one with the characters of his name, as if there were a chance she might think they were from someone else. Unable to find a trash can, she stashed them underneath a defective floor tile in her room; the concrete underneath was sunken like a bowl. By the time he bought a wastepaper basket and placed it at the bottom of the stairs, she'd amassed a collection and thought it would be a shame to throw them away.

At the end of that first week, after he'd laid down fresh carpet in the classrooms and she'd caulked around the bathroom sinks, he drove into Taipei and brought back Peking duck. He showed her the proper way to fold the duck in a pancake with a piece of scallion and sauce. They had a wordless celebration.

Overnight, the school changed from pristine and quiet—just the two of them clicking chopsticks—to being overrun with rambunctious children with runny noses and sticky hands. At first, it was hard to watch the smudges and scuffs that appeared, all the damage tiny hands and feet could inflict. But it was also gratifying to see the results of their hard work put to use. She drew on whiteboards he had hung; his students sat in small chairs she had assembled. Across the hall, he held up a flashcard of a yellow cat she had laminated and his class said C-A-T.

The children loved to touch the hair on her arms, or draw pictures of her with bright green eyes steering a spaceship towards Earth. They were sponges, and could mimic the intonation of her voice exactly within three tries. She said something, they repeated, and they didn't forget. Their parents drilled them at night. By the fourth class, they had mastered animals and colors, and moved on to the rooms of a house, learning at three times the rate she had originally planned. They begged her for English names. She borrowed heavily from the JV field hockey team on which she'd played sophomore year, tossing names out to the kids like chocolate coins. A few times after class she walked outside past the intersection with the intention of searching for the hot springs, but midway there she always found a reason to rush back to the school. Mr. Wang would write down what had happened in her short absence—a plugged-up sink or a new item in the lost-and-found—wielding his pen as if the possibilities were endless.

At night, she and Mr. Wang met at the cardboard box for dinner, exhilarated by their sense of purpose. She showed him a picture one of her students had drawn, a dog with Xs for eyes frying in a pan. Mr. Wang imitated the way his students scratched their heads when they'd forgotten how to spell a word. He scribbled: THERE APPEARED TO BE A MEASLES EPIDEMIC DURING THE MORNING'S QUIZ. He wrote quickly in her presence, sacrificing symmetry for speed.

JACKET OR BLAZER, he wanted to know, producing a flashcard from a folder under his chair.

She wondered if that was what he would wear—an old-school blazer with gold buttons—if he were to take her to a nice restaurant. Or maybe he'd be more comfortable in a white button-down since he didn't seem the type to draw attention to himself.

"Take your pick," she answered. "What difference does it make to a bunch of kids?"

ENORMOUS DIFFERENCE, he insisted, and she couldn't help laugh at the way he'd written the word "enormous," the letters so large they extended across the page. She moved her chair closer to see what came next.

I AM SERIOUS. He added that as teachers, they opened up minds, transformed lives. There was nothing else that left such a mark on the world. One day, when she was older, a former student would come up to her and thank her. Then she would understand the significance of it all.

She read along as he wrote, disappointed when he set down his pen.

"Okay," she said. "I'd go with blazer."

Within days, people were dropping off padded boxes of imported apples and Japanese pears. Someone donated a marble drinking fountain to the school. They received a songbird in a cage, a tin of green bean cakes, a bottle of plum wine. A small truck delivered a pile of painted scrolls. One morning they stepped outside to find roses and orchids planted around the front entrance.

"So many presents!" she said.

THEY CELEBRATE MY SUCCESS.

"How do you know this many people?"

MOST I HAVE NEVER MET.

"Then why do they give you things?"

THERE WAS AN ARTICLE IN THE NEWSPAPER.

That night, they drank the plum wine out of patterned teacups. She showed him how to clink rims and toast.

HOW LONG WILL YOU STAY?

She managed, she thought, to do a reasonable job of describing her situation considering the language barrier. Her ears were bad. Or one was, and the other would soon follow. She would teach for a couple of months until she earned enough money to travel around and experience the world. Then she would return to the States and go deaf.

Even to her, the story sounded false, like one of the far-fetched excuses she'd heard foreigners use—a sudden death in the family, AIDS (if the employer was resistant)—when they were ready to quit and travel again. Two months at the school now seemed pitifully short, barely enough time to remember the kids' names.

She thought he would demand she stay longer. Instead, he wrote, THE TIMING SUITS ME, then wanted to know how much money was enough.

She aimed high, took a stab. "Three thousand US dollars."

He nodded perfunctorily, as though he had arrived at the same figure.

Did he understand? She wasn't sure. He pressed his tooth with his thumb, shook out his hand.

HELEN KELLER, he wrote.

"Well, not exactly," she tried to explain.

He poured another dash of wine into his teacup and slugged it down as if he himself had been handed her diagnosis.

His sister Meimei arrived the following weekend carrying the kind of cheap mesh bag tourists bought when they had too many souvenirs to lug home. It was full of kitchen utensils. She spent all of Saturday in the kitchen, filling the school with smells. First pork, then fish, then sweet bean. Then something fiery that caught in Catherine's throat and made her cough and step outside.

The weather was pleasant, a not-too-hot summer day, and she decided she would take a walk. She didn't make it five yards before the father of a student stopped on his bike to shake her hand. A woman hailed her from across the street. Two students skipped around a yard singing her name. Could she come to their house for lunch? She couldn't remember if it was rude or not to accept. But then she had no choice, because her students pulled her into a small row house also filled with the aroma of cooking. It was the first of three lunches. Afterwards, she was escorted back to the school by a small, exuberant crowd.

A feast awaited her. Meimei, a round-faced girl of eighteen, led her to the makeshift table; she'd turned over three cardboard boxes to accommodate all the food. They both knelt down before eight or so plates, and Meimei put a scoop of rice in a bowl for each of them.

Catherine eyed the food, already stuffed. "Should we wait for Mr. Wang?" she asked.

She could see a sliver of light underneath the kitchen door, the flicker of a shadow, Mr. Wang walking past. The school now smelled of ginger.

Meimei put two flat hands to one side of her cheek. "He will not eat. He rests."

"Do you think he's caught whatever's going around?" A couple of Catherine's students had gone home sick that week.

Meimei nodded, unsure of herself. She pushed a whole fried fish towards Catherine, the eyes an icy blue. Catherine tried to think of a subject they had in common.

"I met Mr. Wang at the market. I don't know much about him."

Meimei had yet to pick up her chopsticks, apparently not hungry either. "He dreamed to be an English teacher since he was a boy. He listened to cassette tapes every night when he went to sleep." She frowned at the pea sprouts. "He is a good brother, a good man, just twenty-four years old. He likes to do everything for himself, but he cannot cook."

"The students like him."

"He was afraid they would laugh."

Catherine heard the water turn on in the kitchen, wondered if Mr. Wang was listening through the door. "Even the first day, the classrooms were overflowing. He had to start a waiting list. Some drove all the way from Taipei."

Meimei stood up when the light in the kitchen went off. "He worried no one would come."

"Can I help you clear the dishes?"

Meimei motioned for Catherine to remain seated. "Please."

Meimei went into the kitchen without turning on the light and shut the door behind her. Catherine stared at the wall; the paint had bubbled up in a few spots but otherwise looked decent. She heard a lone motorcycle roar down the street, the muffler shot. A dog barked. She thought maybe Meimei had gone to bed when Meimei came out carrying a deck of cards.

"Can you play?"

"Sure."

Meimei shuffled the cards. "I will go to nursing school after this."

"I don't know what I want to do."

Meimei looked surprised. "You are a teacher!"

"Right now. But it's not my career."

"Why not?"

"I'm too young to commit myself to any one thing."

Meimei set the deck down between them. "You are very brave!"

They didn't know any of the same games, so Catherine taught Meimei how to play crazy eights. Meimei showed Catherine how to hide cards up her sleeve.

The concierge touched her shoulder. The person she was meeting had arrived, which was strange, because she wasn't meeting anyone. She had made that up so she wouldn't be disturbed. He motioned to the corner of the lobby where a Chinese man sat with his back to her, kneading his knuckles against his lips.

She knew it was a misunderstanding; it was all too familiar. She'd become accustomed to nodding at garbled speech in restaurants, to answering the wrong question, to missing the joke, to people talking into her deaf ear (her husband had complained she purposely turned it towards him). Her kids' friends had imitated her behind her back, tapping a lampshade and saying, "I need to be on your right side to hear you," and, "Could you please face me when you speak?" It felt like half of her was underwater. But she knew how to go through the motions—she was adept at smiling her way through meaningless exchanges—and she would do so now.

She walked across the lobby to the man. "Hello? The concierge said you were looking for me?"

"Oh, I'm sorry. There's been a mix-up. I'm waiting for a different American woman."

"I thought that might be the case."

She gave a small bow and retreated back to her foam seat.

Three weeks later, in the evening, she was taping her students' pictures on the classroom wall when the room began to spin. She clutched the back of the chair she was standing on and screamed. He came running, dropped his masking tape, which looked to her like it rolled up a wall.

He took her in his arms and lifted her off the chair, pinning her hands to her sides, as if he thought she might try to inflict harm on herself. She fell to the floor and he went down with her, angling his body underneath hers to lessen the blow. He tried to make her comfortable, brushing away the hair that stuck to her lips, moving her elbow so it didn't jab her in the side. Then he wrapped himself around her and didn't let go. She lay in his grip, his heart pounding against her back, as the room bucked and swam.

She woke several hours later to darkness and his even breath against her neck. He smelled of scallions and furniture polish; his palms were cool. Her throat felt sore and her cheek was chafed from the rough carpet, but the room was still, upright. She could hear the toilet down the hall, its gurgles and sighs.

She'd lain plenty of times in the arms of a boy, but never under these circumstances. Should she leave? Stay? In any case, she had to use the bathroom. She pried back his fingers and made for the door.

The second-floor bathroom had been designed for the students. She had to squat to reach the toilet seat; the sink came to her thighs.

She ran the hot water and leaned over to let the steam rise to her face. She looked in the mirror: he would call a doctor if he saw her like this. She tried to pinch color into her cheeks, then combed her hair with her fingernails on the way out.

He was awake, standing by the classroom window, looking down onto the street below, holding the slats of the blind apart with his forefinger and thumb. There were no streetlights, but the market had an outside light that gave the intersection a dusky glow. He tugged at the drawstring, showed her it was stuck. Together, they untangled the knots until the blind opened and closed freely, then went their separate ways to catch the last few hours of sleep, as if they often met at night to make minor repairs.

WILL YOU GIVE ME AN ENGLISH NAME? He wrote the following morning at breakfast.

She stood back and nodded, walked a circle around him, made a show of trying to think of a name that fit. She was surprised to catch herself flirting. She thought of Robert first, but she'd had a fling with a Rob once. Same went for Anthony, Tim, Nick, David, John, Peter, Mike, Charles, and most other common American male names that came to mind. They all had associations. It would be unfair to peg him as the captain of the lacrosse team or the dorm proctor or the guy who ate Fruit Loops in the cafeteria alone. Mr. Wang was unlike anyone she had met before.

"How about Dirk?" He was not a Dirk, but it was either that or she'd have to start searching in a different language.

DIRT?

"No, D-I-R-K. Dirk."

He mouthed it to himself, nodded. He wrote it down in his notepad and underlined it twice.

I AM HONORED.

She had the feeling if she'd given him the name Dirt, he would have said the same thing.

"Don't you ever get tired of writing?"

SOMETIMES.

"It takes forever," she said through an exaggerated yawn, surprised—again—to find herself trying to pick a fight.

THANK YOU FOR YOUR PATIENCE. He didn't take the bait.
"You don't need help with your spelling."
I MUST CONTINUE TO PRACTICE.
Later, lying on her tatami, listening to the sound of crickets wafting through her open window, she thought perhaps she would stay longer. As a favor to him.

The following week, on the night her hearing ear started crackling, a noise that in no way could be interpreted as good, she ran downstairs to the kitchen. Mr. Wang was contemplating his notepad, crumpled balls of paper strewn at his feet. He stood up forcefully, toppling his chair. She didn't say anything but he knew. He strode across the room and cupped her ears, pulled her head to his chest.

He held her, stroking her shoulder, her cheek, circling the scar on her chin leftover from a bout of chickenpox. He swayed from side to side, and they began to move around the kitchen. This calmed her down. He seemed to be saying: if this was her moment to go deaf, her ruin, together they would defy it. He eased her down onto his tatami and tucked his body against hers. She reached for his thigh, but he guided her hand away. He breathed with his mouth against the back of her shirt, lulling her to sleep.

In the morning, he put his watch to her good ear and seemed as relieved as she was when she could hear it tick.

She didn't see him the next day, or the one after. There was a sign on the door of the school canceling his classes, and his students went home. Meimei arrived midweek and she and Mr. Wang were holed up in the kitchen, talking in low voices. When Catherine crept downstairs at four in the morning, his light was still on.

"Where's Mr. Wang?" she asked Meimei at dinner the following night. It was a feast again—sesame noodles, egg flower soup, shredded pork, bamboo shoots—as if every night they expected company that never came.

"He rests."

"Again?"

"His neck," Meimei said, brushing the front of her own.

"A sore throat?"

"His hand also."

"Why doesn't he come out?"

"He is—how do you say?—pride."

The kitchen door hadn't opened in two days. Catherine had repeatedly checked the floor around the bulletin board in the hallway, thinking he might have pinned a note for her there that had fallen down.

"Is he avoiding me?"

"He is sick." Meimei accidentally spit out a piece of noodle and put a hand over her mouth.

"He stayed up pretty late last night for being so sick."

"He cannot sleep."

"Do you think he'll teach tomorrow? I'm afraid the students will stop coming if he keeps canceling class."

"They will come."

"I doubt for much longer."

Meimei pushed a bamboo shoot with her chopsticks. She brought it to her mouth, but at the last moment withdrew it. "Where else has no tuition?"

"What do you mean no tuition?"

Meimei tipped her head forward, letting her hair fall over her eyes. "Already, I say too much."

Meimei wanted to play crazy eights after dinner, but first she had to run out to buy MSG at the market before it closed. Catherine waited until she left before knocking on the kitchen door.

"What's going on around here? Open up!"

No answer. She thought she heard a sound like rustling leaves.

"Classes are free?" she said. "What kind of school is this? Why did you bring me out here in the first place?"

Again, rustling.

"You said you'd pay me three thousand dollars."

The fridge clicked on, an unsteady, wavering hum.

"I know you're in there."

She was getting ready to barge in when the door opened. He stood there swallowing, holding his throat, a diminished, less nourished version of himself. His eyes searched hers for something—understanding? compassion?—or perhaps just to gauge the truth of what she saw.

He fumbled with a slip of paper, tried to write something down, but his hand wouldn't cooperate, wouldn't hold still. She realized she hadn't heard him speak in weeks. She slapped the pen out of his hand.

"No, tell me to my face," she said. "You owe me at least that!"

He slurred something unintelligible, saliva coating his lips, swung his head in the direction of a thick envelope lying on the counter near the sink. Even from the hall, she could tell there was more than three thousand dollars inside. He stumbled across the kitchen to retrieve it; she couldn't bear to watch. For a moment, she imagined throwing herself at his feet, but then shut the door and left, as if he were just another boyfriend who had fallen out of grace.

This time it was the man nudging her. He thought he'd recognized her. Had she ever lived in this town?

She said she had a long time ago.

Was she an English teacher?

Not now. But before, yes.

The man sat down across from her and folded his hands, looking like the bearer of bad news. He had the kind of intrusive mustache that made lip-reading difficult.

"I was a student of yours."

"Oh?"

"You gave me the English name—what was it?—Bernie."

"How awful. I don't know what I was thinking."

"Then you don't mind that I changed it?"

"God, no."

"I always felt guilty."

"Please don't. What is it now?"

"Ben."

"Much better. It suits you."

The man looked pleased. "Do you remember me?"

She nodded vaguely, picturing a group of kids sucking on blood Popsicles before class. Their red mouths had sickened her at first— it looked like they'd been gorging on raw flesh—but after a while, she'd learned to pretend it was cherry or grape. Was Bernie the one who had lice? The one who'd lost his tooth in a steamed bun? Or maybe that was all of them, one and the same.

"What happened to the school?" she said.

"Changed hands a couple times, torn down, and now this. What brings you back?"

"I left the school in a hurry, forgot some things."

The man looked around, amused. "You weren't expecting to find them, were you?"

"I don't know what I expected. Probably not."

"You did leave rather abruptly, I remember. After six weeks?"

"I returned home." She reluctantly took out her earplug; she'd wanted to take a break from listening—it was a constant strain with one ear—but the man wouldn't quit and the mustache was throwing her off.

"You don't like the music?" he laughed, pointing up to the speaker as a clash of cymbals broke in.

"My ears are very sensitive," she said, stupidly. You told people you were part deaf, and they'd holler about a sister confined to a wheel-chair or a widower uncle who'd gone blind, as if to remind you that purgatory was better than hell.

The man lifted a clenched hand to his mouth, as if to cough, but didn't. "You knew he had Lou Gehrig's disease?" he said, touching his lip. "His parents bought him the school so he could live out his dream before, you know..."

"I knew he was sick."

"He was embarrassed by his voice. His speech became impaired. It didn't take long for the rest to follow."

"I'm sorry to hear that."

"There was a rumor he ran off with you and opened a new school."

"No."

"I believed it, anyway. Even after I knew the truth. It's funny, I still have to catch myself."

A blond woman arrived, and the man introduced her as his fiancée. He'd met her online. "All because I had a great English teacher," the man said, flourishing a hand at Catherine. They were planning on having their wedding banquet at the hotel. They were late for a meeting with the chef to finalize the menu.

The wedding was only a week away, but would Catherine be able to attend?

She would not. She had to get back to the tour group—and, of course—to her kids, her job, to finalize her divorce, to the accrual of mundane problems unimaginable to her the last time she was here.

In the end, she called her parents for help and they wired her the money to come home. She finished college, dating the roommate of her ex-boyfriend senior year. She learned sign language—to hedge her bets—and got a degree in speech-language pathology. She was paired with Bobby Anderson in a mixed-doubles tennis tournament one summer and married him the next. The doctors were wrong: the hearing in her good ear fluctuated over the years but never left. She vigilantly protected what she had with earplugs. She worked part-time and had kids. She'd been impatient with them at times, but she'd also been there for every musical performance, every game, once stopping up her younger son's bloody nose with a new silk blouse. She'd been known—after a few drinks—to sing karaoke every so often.

There were times her tinnitus got so bad, it kept her up at night.

Awake at night, she sometimes thought about him, wishing she'd stayed, but what was the use?

She'd made whatever she'd made of herself. That part was done.

She packed her green knapsack, ran out the front door, and bumped into Meimei on her way back from the market, nearly knocking her into a rose bush. She thought Meimei might try to stop her, but instead she wordlessly dropped her bag of groceries, led her out into the intersection, and helped her flag down a passing bus.

The girls at the hostel were different, but the same. They shuffled cards on their bunks and took turns cutting the deck. The Danish woman had returned after a short modeling stint, for which she hadn't been paid, and was looking for more work. She sat on her cot, clipping her nails.

"That man from the street market? I remember he gave you that money up front. What did he want from you?"

"It was a school," Catherine mumbled.

"Did you sleep with him?"

"It wasn't like that."

The girls gave her sympathetic nods. "Of course not," they said. "Try not to think about it too much."

They moved their card game over to her bunk, consoling her, saying how sorry they were to see her go.

I wasn't even out of baggage claim when I spotted my brother, Doug, with the same old scraggly beard, slumped across a row of plastic chairs, mouth open, eyes rolled back into his head.

I grabbed my backpack off the carousel and walked over to him. "You could get arrested for that."

He jumped up, did some kind of pretend split in the air. "Surprise!"

In the Chevy, on the way to his place, he gave me the rundown: our parents still lived in the same RV resort, playing shuffleboard even though half the time they used the wrong end of the cue. Buster, who'd been born six weeks premature, was growing like a kangaroo. Dina had started drinking coffee again even though it gave her an overactive bladder; she was excited to finally meet me.

"Oh, and I work the night shift at 7-Eleven now," Doug said, pointing to himself and nodding. "Goodbye, stand-up. Hello, Big Gulp. Got bills to pay, you know?" He told me he'd already gained ten pounds.

I told him after being gone for so long, American food gave me heartburn. I couldn't get used to all the cell phones; I kept interrupting people's conversations, assuming they were talking to me. And the clothes people wore were so bright, I had to shield my eyes. I didn't think I could go back to my old job, the one where I organized people's closets. If I saw fifty pairs of shoes in one place, I'd probably freak. Before I left for India, I'd sold off everything I owned—including a stereo and a leopard gecko—that didn't fit into my backpack.

"Bottom line," I said, "I'm not the person I was before."

"You're my sister," Doug said. "Last time I saw you, you had this trick where you made snide comments about people without moving your lips." He tried to show me, talking out the side of his mouth.

"I did?"

"And you had a crush on that guy—what was his name?—Ricky or Rambo? He'd get into those bar brawls and the only way to sober him up was to hose him off in the parking lot."

I had vague recollection of a well-developed biceps encircled by a tentacle tattoo, but that was about it.

"Nobody's themselves anymore," Doug said, shaking his head. He drove with his thumb and forefinger, pinching the wheel. "Why would a customer use Chapstick on his eyebrows? Why do bald people buy shampoo?"

I shrugged my shoulders but I didn't know if he could see.

"Take me," he said. "I'm a comedian but I stand behind a counter giving out the key to the restroom. I see a guy, and I know how long it takes him to go shit." He seemed to be concentrating on something, the road, I hoped. "Anyway, we need to make up for lost time."

For the past four years, I'd sent him postcards. I described working for Mother Teresa: the never-ending defecation, the twitching limbs. For his amusement, I mentioned a temple where monkeys steal the sunglasses right off your face. I explained how my boyfriend John and I lived in Goa for a while, juggling on the beach and sanding coconut bowls. We made jewelry and sold it at the market on Wednesdays. Every week or so I stuck a postcard in the mail, writing a couple of lines each time.

My brother wrote about his and Dina's wedding (shotgun) in front of the orangutang cage at the zoo. The orangutangs celebrated by ripping up magazines and doing a little dance. When Buster was born, Doug sent me a lock of his hair. What could we say? I was in India and he was in Oregon. I gave him the basics: He knew I lived in dirt-cheap guesthouses and worked here and there to get by. He was familiar with the story of how I met John.

John was the only other foreigner on a bus to Jaipur and we nodded at each other through swaying bodies in the aisle. I was sitting in back, squeezed in between five men, when one next to me put his hand on my knee and said, "You are all alone?" I felt the hair rise on the back of my neck. Before I could answer, there was a tall figure standing over us, a scar across his chin like a third lip, saying, "Would you mind switching seats so I can sit next to my wife?"

But there were other things, things my own brother didn't know.

. . .

When Doug introduced me to Dina, she was wearing a neon-or-
ange sweater that went down to her knees. She had braces and chewed
nonstick gum; she worked as a dental assistant so she got them for
free. "Hey there!" she said, popping a bubble between her teeth. I
followed her into the living room, where she gave me the lay of the
land: a TV that needed to be banged three times, a brown couch that
made you cough because it smelled of Doug's feet, and a rag rug that
was good for mopping up spills. There was one chair, a wooden one,
where visitors usually sat. She handed me a mold of her mouth made
three years ago, teeth huddled together as if from the cold. I pulled
the wax tongue out and stuck it back in.

We sat in the living room before Doug went to work. There were
three small sausage dogs that sniffed me and yawned. Dina turned
on the TV, banging it, but kept the volume low. She sat on the floor
close up because her ears were clogged. My brother stretched out on
the couch, his long toes pointing up. When he picked his nose, not
paying attention, Dina turned around and asked him, "Digging for
gold?"

When Buster woke up from his nap, they shot it out, played two
out of three to see who got the baby. My brother lost. He went out
and came back with Buster, saying, "Little Mister is hungry." He fed
Buster a bottle, telling me, "At first, we didn't know what we were
doing. We still don't." Buster had a widow's peak like a wizened old
man. Doug and Dina were going to give him a cane for Halloween
and call it good. During TV commercials, Doug moved Buster's legs
around so he was bicycling the air. Doug's shift didn't start until
eleven o'clock at night.

We watched a show about how to avoid being mugged if you're
walking down the street. There were three criminals with short
spiky hair sitting in director's chairs giving advice, saying things like,
"Whatever you do, do not accept a piece of chocolate from a strang-
er," and "Be careful not to aim the pepper spray into your own eyes."
Doug and Dina thought this was funny, flopping and rolling like fish
on the floor.

"There were robbers in India," I said. "Thieves all around."

Doug climbed back up on the couch and looked at me. "Dina, should we tell her?" he said.

I bit some skin around my thumbnail and said, "Tell me what?"

Doug explained he and Dina were forever making bets. They bet on whether Ma will call 9-1-1 again the next time her dentures fall in the toilet, or how old Buster will be when he can finish a Big Mac. If the phone rings, they guess which creditor it is. Just before I came back, they bet on things like if I'd remember how to eat with utensils and whether I'd have weird streaks of makeup on my cheeks.

"We thought you might walk through the front door wearing a sorcerer's hat," Doug said.

I sat on the wooden chair waving as if I were in a parade, then folded my hands and tucked them under my chin. I didn't like the attention being on me. "Well, as a matter of fact," I said, "there was an incident."

"But you're all right," Doug said, extracting lint from his beard. "You're wearing jeans. You're speaking English. You don't have nineteen pigtails sticking out of your head."

We watched TV until my brother went to work. After he left, Dina got ready for bed, walking through the house, turning off the lights. I heard her clothes rustle when she climbed the stairs. I lay on the brown couch in the living room and coughed, listening to the ticking of the TV. It ticked for about ten minutes, cooling down, before it went silent.

It felt strange to be alone when only days before I'd been part of a team. John and I took turns scrounging for food and finding places to sleep. On buses, John opened his eyes every ten minutes or so, keeping watch over me, sometimes through the night. Each of us made sure the other was drinking enough water. When John got typhoid, I brought him, practically carried him, to a doctor. I depended on him and he depended on me.

I walked around the downstairs with my flashlight, circling from the kitchen to the living room and down the hall and back to the kitchen. I touched dried flowers and picked up junk mail. I slid across the kitchen floor in my socks. Doug brought home the expired food from 7-Eleven so the fridge was stocked. To soften the bread I had to toast it.

· · ·

During breakfast, Buster sat in a swing and tracked Doug with his eyes when Doug walked to the sink. Dina sliced the butter sideways, running the knife along the top and leaving grooves. She folded her bread in half.

"Does Buster want to lie on the floor?" Dina said, taking a small, checkered quilt out of a closet. Buster was quiet in his little green cabbage pajamas so Dina turned to Doug and said, "Is he a vegetable or what?"

My brother tapped his foot underneath the table and said, "When you're at work today I'm going to take Little Mister and Sister to feed the ducks." He pointed at me and added, "Just like when we were kids." He drank coffee with NoDoz, pinching Dina in the side, saying, "Please tell me it's your turn to give Buster Boy a bath."

Besides bread and butter, they offered me Pop-Tarts. In between trips to the bathroom, chugging coffee there and back, Dina asked me, "So what do they eat in India?" A rubber band flew out of her mouth and landed on the table. "Sorry," she said, then picked up the rubber band, all stretched out and broken, and set it to the side of her plate.

"They eat thalis, dosas, samosas," I answered, throwing out names without explaining them, then added, "but there's a kind of yogurt drink you might like."

When I went to stick my Pop-Tart in the toaster, I heard Dina whisper, "Weird stuff."

"Shh," my brother said. "Just say it's normal."

Near the fridge, there was an old tub with claw feet. I crouched down next to it and said, "One time when John and I were eating breakfast at a hostel, the manager came over and sat down at our table. He secretly unwrapped a tiger paw from a white cloth and said, 'For you, my friends, I give special price.'"

"That's disgusting," Dina said, sticking her finger in her mouth.

Doug closed his eyes. "I'm trying to picture it," he said. But then he opened them and pointed to the tub: "That's where we make our home brew."

Dina went upstairs to get her coat and Doug shouted after her, "Release the hounds!" The three of them came yapping out of their cages. Dina came back down and stood in the middle of the kitchen, picking her lip, watching the dogs sniff Buster and trot around. The dogs had never hurt Buster—they usually tried to lick him clean— but still, Dina said, you never knew. Once, one of them pushed his food bowl in between the stove and the fridge and growled at Dina when she went to slide it out. She couldn't even open the fridge to get something for herself. She had to wait until the dog calmed down and went outside. Another time, one of the dogs took my brother's sock and wouldn't give it back. Doug followed the dog from room to room while it slunk from one hiding place to another.

"We found the dogs kind of random," Dina said.

"Hey," Doug said, snapping his fingers, "kind of the same way you found John."

In Varanasi, John and I juggled in the street and carried each other piggyback up and down the ghats. We spoke to each other in pig Latin. I pretended to faint in public, knowing John would be there to catch me in the nick of time. John liked to choke in restaurants to get us free meals. We lived on forty dollars a week. We laughed, saying things like, "So much for working in a cubicle" or "If only my tenth-grade teacher could see me now." In a dingy room with a view out onto the Ganges, John said, "People back home wouldn't understand." "Yup," I answered, proud, "no one else would get this, get us." We watched a pod of freshwater dolphins leap past a painted rowboat.

Doug looked at Dina and she shifted her weight onto one leg.

"But I've seen shows where a dog saves a baby's life in a fire or rescues a baby drowning in a pool," she said. "Most dogs turn out all right in the end."

She buttoned her coat, getting ready for the office. She walked out the door and shouted back: "You wouldn't believe the things I see every day! Some people have shark teeth! Others grow fangs!"

On the wall in my brother and Dina's room there are posters of dressed-up dangling chimpanzees saying things like, Thought I'd drop in and Mind if I hang around? You can find a plastic milk crate filled with *Mad* magazines, a hand buzzer, glue-on mustaches, and trick gum. The dogs' cages are lined up under the window, labeled Dumb, Dumber, and Complete Dumbass. Dina has a pink bottle of perfume called Wonderstruck.

Buster's room has a towel-rug in the shape of a smiley face. In the corner, there's a diaper bin that gets jammed unless you pick it up and drop it. A rocking chair is piled high with carnival winnings, beanbag penguins and a giant snake.

Dina keeps little packets of rubber bands in the bathroom on the side of the sink. I sprayed some of my brother's shaving cream and played with the faucets, turning the water on and off. I read the directions on a bottle of lotion. Things were starting to come back.

In the living room, there's a wedding picture of Dina, hair in an updo, braces flashing, pretending to run from the cheetah pacing behind the glass. In the bathroom, there's a picture of Buster taking a bath in the sink, staring down a rubber duck. The three dogs are dressed as ZZ Top, with beards and hats, in a picture in Buster's room. Near the front door, there's one of Doug sitting in Santa's lap as a grown adult, a line of kids waiting. In the hall, Doug and I are teenagers riding bikes with clown horns. We used to honk at cars and make them wait while we took forever to cross the road.

When I decided to leave India, my boyfriend, John, gave me a picture from Pushkar. In it, I'm riding on a camel. My hair is matted and I have a scab on my lip. "There's no going back, not like this," he said, his scar a second smile. He traced my crooked face in the picture, stopping at the eyes with their drooping lids.

"I have to," I said. That same day John had pickpocketed a fellow traveler and emptied the contents of the wallet out onto our mattress. He said it was just another one of our games. He plucked a condom from a pile of coins and looked at the expiration date. I thought of the way Doug and I used to dump out our bags of Halloween candy, checking for holes in the wrappers. What do you do with a memory like that? I just knew it was time to head home.

John wasn't happy that I was leaving after four years. He was desperate. He stuck the picture in my face, saying, "People will run for the hills."

When we got ready to feed the ducks, my brother grabbed some old bread from the fridge and called the dogs. He put a snowflake snowsuit on Buster and waited for me at the door. When Buster turned bright red Doug said, "Little Mister's overheating," singing a warning. He called the dogs out of their cages and lifted Buster up against his shoulder and we stepped outside.

The pond was a two-minute walk away. Doug gave me the leashes to hold and we walked in the middle of the road so the dogs wouldn't get muddy. Buster smacked his lips, but other than that the only sound was the wind shaking the leaves.

"Did you ever have a major lapse in judgment?" I asked Doug, acting casual, letting my sneakers drag on the ground.

He stopped and tapped his foot, puffing his cheeks with air. "Let me think." He told me about the time he put a dog in the baby carriage and strolled around the park.

There were about fifty ducks in the pond and they all came rushing over when they saw us. My brother chuckled, taking the bread out of the bag, saying, "Everybody in the neighborhood feeds them. They already know." The ducks came close, but not too close because of the dogs. I stood back a little, holding the leashes, thinking, Now this is normal. There is probably nothing more normal than feeding ducks. Then Doug said, "Watch out!" He lobbed a big hunk of bread and the ducks charged over, flapping and fighting.

I watched Doug kiss Buster's head. Buster's hair was floating up, as if magnetically drawn to the sky. I put my hands in my pockets and hunched my shoulders, then stood straight up with my arms hanging down. "Have you ever lost your mind?" I said.

Doug hopped on one foot to jog his memory. He walked around in circles, fast, eyes on the ground. He handed me Buster and said: "Reel in the hounds!"

In the middle of all the ducks, there was one that was speckled. "Take note," Doug said, showing me how the speckled duck could catch pieces of bread in its bill. Doug made a trail of bread away from the pond and most of the ducks followed until they got to the road. But when the other ducks turned back, the speckled one didn't.

The speckled duck trailed behind Doug making little peeping noises, picking up the small balls of bread that Doug rolled between his palms and dropped. "Come on, Daffy," Doug said, "don't let me down now." And the duck didn't. Sometimes it looked around, or ruffled out its wings and tucked them back in, but still it kept following. When a car passed by, Doug held up his hand as if to say, *Make way for the VIP.* The duck ran off into the bushes but then came back. "That's it," Doug said, "you can do it." And this duck waddled all the way up the road and into Doug's house. I tied the dogs outside and went in to find my brother sitting on the couch in the living room, using the phone. The duck was quacking louder now, sounding the alarm.

"Oh, Dina," Doug said into the receiver, "we have an unexpected guest." He put the receiver next to the duck so Dina could hear the commotion. Hanging up the phone, he said, "Dina said I'm out of control."

I wanted Doug to understand that I was talking about crossing a line, reaching a point of no return.

So I put Buster down and got the picture of me riding that camel from my backpack and handed it to him. I thought he should know. From where I stood, I looked very small in the picture. In fact, I looked more like a drunk child. But my brother didn't do that act where he pretends to have a heart attack and gives himself chest compressions. Or the one where he has butter fingers or the ground beneath him is ice. Instead, he walked around, looking at the walls, examining every detail. He went into the kitchen and I followed him, the duck honking behind. He turned around several times then shuffled over and pulled a magnet off the fridge door.

"Here," he said. "I found a place."

The Enchanted Inn

They were the grand-prize winners of a weekend for four at the Enchanted Inn, where the kids could buy magic wands at the gift shop. The wands made Secret Magic Objects talk and light up. Everyone had been there except them, all thirty-five kids in Jackson's first-grade class. There'd been a one-time cheapo Groupon deal, rumored to be a glitch in the system, and ever since, Jackson's classmates had been bringing in Great Enchanted paraphernalia—fake medallions and crystals—every Friday for show-and-tell. Then one Thursday evening, just as Jackson was throwing his fossil collection across the room and flushing the rare stamps from his grandfather down the toilet, they got a call from the Little League coach informing them they held the winning raffle ticket.

The four of them were: Jackson, Ella, Jeanne, and Rick. Jackson had been begging to go on a Great Enchanted Quest for two years; he was left-handed and tended to fixate on things. Ella, their oblivious four-year-old, was happy anywhere she could run laps. Rick and Jeanne, the parents, had met fifteen years earlier in Bali. Rick had been attending a mask-carving workshop, Jeanne studying coral reefs. They'd shacked up together in a cliff-top villa with a view of the Indian Ocean, living like royalty, with a staff that was—if not serving them—endlessly polishing the furniture and mopping the tile floors. Jeanne and Rick had eaten jumbo prawns every day, sitting on their private frangipani-adorned patio, all paid for by Jeanne's modest graduate school stipend.

Now they were in their mid-forties—lost in dirty laundry, battling allergies to mold and household dust—feeling too tired to run after Ella and deal with Jackson's night-before-show-and-tell tantrums. Their year hadn't been great. Jackson had crashed his secondhand bike with the faulty wheel (Jeanne had been kicking herself ever since for not buying him a new one) and broken his arm and it was never going to look the same. Ella's pre-K teacher was pressuring them to put Ella on Adderall. Rick's masks had been displayed at Bob's Coffee for the past six months without a single sale, and Jeanne felt trapped as a biology instructor at the local community college. The hot-water heater in their two-bedroom starter house had been leaking for a month but they didn't have the money for a new one. Ditto for the roof. So this trip, a weekend at the Enchanted Inn, with the kids happily occupied, the first chance since Bali to kick back on someone else's dime, had come at the perfect moment.

During the hour-long car ride, the kids didn't fight. They actually shared a Lego catalog, making Rick and Jeanne up front exchange sideways are-those-our-children glances. Upon arrival, after pushing their way through a crowd of kids surrounding an adult princess, after waiting in line for half an hour at the reception desk while unattended toddlers squawked and shrieked, they were upgraded for free to a Magic Family Bunk Room, which came with a Magic Bunkbed for the kids, when originally they would have had to all cram together in a king-size bed. They were also eligible for four free meals at the brunch buffet while their room was "repaired," whatever that meant. They could store their luggage behind the front desk. "Enchanted," said the desk clerk, a grown woman in braces, giving them four glossy vouchers and pointing them to the Spellbound Cafeteria.

Normally the kids would have freaked out at the wait—five minutes without full-on entertainment was a tragedy—but the fact that the cereal bar had dispensers with not only Frosted Flakes, but gummy bears, M&M's and Oreo Pieces made up for it. The kids went crazy, filling up their bowls, wondering whether or not they were obligated to add milk. At one point, Jeanne had imagined raising her kids on organic free-range chicken and quinoa, but their budget was more along the lines of Kraft macaroni and cheese. She'd also wanted her kids to speak a second language, but there were no language classes at her son's school. The district could barely afford soap. When Jeanne volunteered in her son's overcrowded classroom once a month, the teacher seemed to spend most of the time trying to get the students to stay in their seats. It was like Whac-A-Mole, students constantly popping up to get snacks, or have outbursts, or look out the window, or, once when Jeanne was there, to sprint—unsuccessfully—to the bathroom. Jeanne had taken the poor soiled kid to the main office to clean up and get a change of clothes from the lost-and-found, telling herself they needed to find a way to move to an area with better schools.

Rick managed to flag down the one waitress, with snarled gray hair in pigtails, to order coffee. Jackson finished his bowl of M&M's, left the table, and returned with two premade chocolate-coated ice-cream cones. He handed one to Ella. Jeanne's horror was slightly abated by the fact that he was sharing. Around them, children with chocolate mustaches had tantrums, hitting their parents with their magic wands. The waitress returned without coffee, plunking down two unordered cartoon cups of soda in front of the kids.

"Whoa there," Rick said, reaching for the cups, but Jackson—quick on the draw—picked his up, turned his back, and began sucking it down. Ella copied her brother.

Rick closed his eyes, took advantage of the free moment. "I need a new career," he said. The only time he and Jeanne could have a conversation was when the kids were eating something they weren't allowed to or watching TV.

"What do you mean?" Jeanne asked. She had to be careful; Rick was touchy about his art. He went through phases where he said he was giving it up but never followed through. She'd always find him a week or two later in their garage, his studio, hands flecked with clay, shrugging his shoulders, sheepish. In Bali, they'd taken an oath to remain true to themselves, their science, their art, no matter what happened in life, and he always mentioned this as the factor that brought him back.

"Bob from Bob's Coffee called. He wants me to come take down my masks."

"There are plenty of other coffee shops that would be happy to display your work. What about Raincity Coffee? Last time I was in there, they had batik from this village in Africa." Jeanne had offered reassurance many times before, and meant it, but now it rang hollow, probably because of Jackson's arm, which might be looking normal if they'd had the resources to go above and beyond their insurance plan into the realm of plastic surgery. If Jackson were, say, one of Angelina Jolie's kids, guaranteed the arm would be looking just fine.

Sodas drunk, Jackson and Ella turned back around and chanted, "Three-day weekend!" over and over, because that's what they said whenever they were with their parents in a location other than home. It was something Jackson had picked up at school.

"Let's say Raincity takes the masks," Rick said. "Let's say I get lucky and sell one. No, let's say it's a miracle and I sell two. That's four hundred dollars. I mean, we need a new roof."

"But you can't just give up."

This, of course, begged the question of whether Jeanne herself had given up. Looking in from the outside, one would have said no. She loved biology and was able to teach it. But the reality was Jeanne spent a majority of her time on e-mail dealing with students flaking out on assignments and labs and claiming her instructions were unclear, students missing exams, students contesting their grades. She'd had to dumb down her classes year after year to match the caliber of the incoming freshmen. She thought she could remain a biologist, but the connection between Bali—snorkeling the whole day and taking notes on the behavior of cardinalfish—and what she currently did was becoming more and more remote.

She was kidding herself. It was nonexistent.

"I want a wand," Jackson said, when one landed on their table, overturning the salt.

"Wand! Wand! Wand!" Ella said.

Jeanne was disappointed to watch a puffy-faced father pick up the wand from the middle of their table, without apology, without eye contact, and hand it back to his chubby androgynous child. That was one of the problems with the West Coast: there were lower standards. Rick and Jeanne were transplants from the East Coast; they'd moved to a hip Oregon town so Rick could make his masks without anyone—mostly his former high-school classmates, who were doctors and lawyers—making fun of him.

"But what if I'm a crappy artist?" Rick said. "What if my stuff is terrible? What if nobody's told me all these years?"

"But it's not. You know it's not. Even that guy from that gallery liked it."

"Then why isn't he showing my work?"

"Buy a wand! Buy a wand!" Jackson and Ella were making a song of it now, to the painful tune of some Disney movie, probably *Frozen*.

The kids did not do well on sugar. Jeanne estimated they'd each just ingested about ninety-five grams. At home, Jeanne allowed them two graham crackers and a glass of juice a day, but it seemed a losing battle when sugar was added to everything including bread. She tried not to picture the cell damage taking place, glucose molecules sticking to proteins.

"Just wait until Mom and I get our coffees," Rick said. "Then we can head to the gift shop."

But it was as if he had said, "On your mark, get set, go!" Jackson and Ella sprang up from the table and ran for the door.

Your Magic Wand

The gift shop sold Regular Wands, which were brown, and Premium Wands, which were two to three times more expensive and came in shiny colors. Jackson and Ella immediately went for the shiny ones—what kid wouldn't?—Jackson's striped blue, and Ella's gold with tassels.

"Hold on," Rick said, "we're getting the least expensive ones. We're not spending a fortune here."

The kids clung tightly to their Premium Wands, ready to make a scene.

"Hand them over," Rick said. "Right now."

The kids weren't budging.

"Jeanne," Rick said, "I need some backup here."

Jeanne felt for the kids. They were always getting secondhand stuff—thus the crooked bicycle wheel, Jackson's bike accident, etc.—always wearing clothes frayed at the cuffs. They'd never skied. Everything was too expensive, that was all they ever heard. Rick would never understand because he'd grown up with—no kidding—a Shetland pony. They'd kept it at a stable in Bridgehampton, where he summered. His parents spoiled him until he graduated from RISD and betrayed them by moving west. But Jeanne had vivid memories of being the only girl in her class not wearing a pair of Guess jeans on a field trip to The Cloisters and it had scarred her for life.

"Let's just let them get the Premium Wands," Jeanne said.

"Are you getting a raise?" Rick said. "Because I'm not." To support his art, Rick worked as an activity coordinator at an assisted-living facility. Once a week, he taught the seniors wheel-throwing techniques.

"The regular ones look like they're made out of dung. People are going to think they're carrying…" It was highway robbery, the way they'd turned "regular" into "inferior" everywhere you went, so that you either had to suffer humiliation or go over your credit limit.

"Mommy, what's dung?" Ella said.

"Okay, then you deal with this," Rick said. "I'm losing patience. I'm going to Starbucks."

He stepped across the hallway to the Starbucks and got in the end of a long line in which everyone was wearing plaid. It looked like he was part of a tour group, the plaid and sneakers club, although Rick's shirt was more fitted than the rest, a vestige of his New York upbringing. Still, he'd gotten sloppier over the years.

"It's poop," said Jackson, who'd just finished a farm unit in school. "Dung means poop."

"Okay, Jackson, that's enough," Jeanne said.

"Jackson said poop! Jackson said poop!" Ella sang.

Some kid—thankfully not Jeanne's, not this time—dashed into the gift shop in a wet bathing suit, brandishing an Ultra Premium Wand, which resembled a lightsaber, and dripping water on the floor. He sliced the wand in the direction of his brother, who was chasing him, knocking a shelf of gnomish figurines to the floor. The two of them ran out, leaving puddles.

The guy behind the cash register looked up from sorting plastic medallions and runes into tubs.

"Enchanted," he said.

"Not my kid," Jeanne said. "That wasn't my kid." She was almost giddy with relief; her children weren't the only nightmare around.

But then Ella scratched Jackson on the face, drawing blood. Why? Because Ella was a baby owl who had just hatched and Jackson didn't feed her a mouse fast enough and Ella had talons.

Jeanne often found herself inviting her kids to join her in the real world.

Jackson howled.

The guy at the register did not shake his head or make disapproving clicking noises, even when Ella let out one of her fingernails-on-a-chalkboard screeches. The staff at the Enchanted Inn had apparently received some kind of intense training that enabled them to go about their jobs unaffected by the most severe of tantrums, as though inoculated against disease. The guy continued to sort plastic crap as if it were a form of meditation. Jeanne tried to view her kids with the same detached calmness, but all she could see was Jackson and Ella ten years down the road, addicted to drugs, in jail.

Jeanne slapped forty dollars on the counter—she carried cash for this purpose—and left the shop without collecting her change. Rick, the self-appointed coupon-cutter and model of frugality, would have wanted the four dollars back, but Rick was in line at Starbucks, across the hall, spending four dollars on a coffee.

So they were even. So there.

Hidden Treasure

After returning to the gift shop to get the wands powered up (that was the problem with quick exits, you always had to return), the kids shot off into the lobby, running around and shaking their wands at Secret Magic Objects. There was a bear rug whose eyes turned red, and a wooden macaque that swung back and forth in a cage over the reception desk. The fireplace sputtered and lit up. A statue of a fairy cackled. Paintings thundered out nonsensical riddles. Jeanne tried not to think about the hair cells in her kids' cochleae, how many were being killed off. Maybe stem-cell scientists would figure out a way to regenerate human hair cells by the time the kids were grown, otherwise, with all the prevalent noise pollution, especially surrounding kids' activities, they'd need hearing aids by the age of forty-five.

Down a hall, they reached a treasure chest. It took both kids tapping their wands together to open it, revealing what looked like rock candy inside. A voice boomed from a hidden speaker: "The treasure shalt be thine if thee dare to embark upon the Great Enchanted Quest!" Jeanne tried to get her kids to cover their ears.

"Let's go on the Great Enchanted Quest," Jackson said. "Can we? Can we?" He thrust his wand at the ceiling, but his bad arm didn't fully straighten anymore. It made the gesture look feeble.

"Quests are expensive," Jeanne said. She'd seen a menu above the counter at the gift shop; they were asking fifty bucks a pop for a basic quest, an arm and a leg. She was scared to find out what the Great Enchanted Quest cost.

"But we're not paying for the room," Jackson said. "We didn't pay for breakfast."

Jeanne wondered why Ella was not chiming in, then saw her hunched over in a corner, throwing up into the pot of a fake palm tree.

"That is why we cannot have gummy bears and ice cream for breakfast," Jeanne said, walking over to Ella, searching her purse for baby wipes.

"I'm bored," Ella said, standing up, vomit dribbling down her jumpsuit.

"Yeah, we've already done everything with the wands," Jackson said. "Except a quest. If you go on the Great Enchanted Quest, you get diamonds and stuff."

"We need to find Daddy," Jeanne said. "Ella needs a change of clothes."

"I don't want to change my clothes," Ella said. "I like my clothes." She was wearing her favorite outfit, a Hello Kitty one-piece, size 2T, busting at the seams.

Jeanne marched off in the direction of Starbucks, with the kids, she hoped, in tow. She envisioned Rick letting people cut in front of him, biding his kid-free time.

Rick wasn't at the Starbucks, so they combed the lobby, the kids flicking their wands at everything, including passersby. A stuffed owl spun its head around three-hundred-and-sixty degrees. A pinball machine played by itself. They ended up standing outside the men's room. Jeanne sent Jackson inside to look.

"He's in there!" Jackson said, coming out. "He's in there!"

"Okay, let's give him a few minutes of privacy."

"He's just staring at his coffee."

"What?"

"He's standing by the mirror, staring at his coffee."

"Then tell him to come out."

Jackson looped back in and reappeared. "He locked himself in a stall. He said he wants a minute to himself."

"Is there anyone else in there?"

"I don't know."

"Go check."

Jackson returned saying there was no one else inside.

"You and Ella stay right here and don't move."

Jeanne walked into the men's room, into the stench of urinal cakes. Rick was in the last stall. She could see his sneakers, the familiar specks of paint. She stood in front of the bolted door.

"Rick? What are you doing?"

"Can't I just have a moment, Jeanne? I haven't finished a complete thought in seven years."

"Ella threw up all over herself and we need to get the luggage so she can change. I can't carry the suitcase with my back."

"I'm having a crisis here, Jeanne. I'm done with my masks."

"But you can't just—"

"I'm not giving up. I'm being practical. All I'm asking for is thirty seconds here to grieve."

"Okay, okay," Jeanne said, backing out of the restroom.

But then Ella bounded in, sidling past her. She waved her wand at a toilet, trying to make it flush.

"It's not working!" she said. "It's not working!"

"Ella, sweetie, I don't think toilets are Secret Magic Objects."

"They are," Ella wailed, crumpling to the floor. "Jackson said they are."

Rick pushed his way out of the stall. "Jackson, get in here! If you told your sister toilets are magic, then you need to show her how."

Jackson stepped into the restroom with one eyebrow raised, something he was proud of because Rick couldn't do it. Rick couldn't even wink. Jackson crinkled his nose when the urinal stench hit.

He walked over to Ella and gently pried the tasseled wand from her hand. "Now watch carefully," he said.

He waved a wand at the toilet three times and stomped his foot.

"It didn't flush," Ella sniffled. "It still didn't flush."

"It's not supposed to flush, silly," Jackson said, eyeing the toilet. "Come here."

He and Ella stood over the toilet, peering in.

"Do you see what I see?" he said.

Ella squinted.

"Look closely."

Ella bent down, face in the bowl.

"Sea monkeys?" she said.

"Bingo!"

"What do they eat?"

"What do you think they eat?"

He gave Ella the wide-eyed look that meant they should keep the answer to themselves because adults in all their lameness would never understand.

"For real life?" Ella said.

"For real life," Jackson answered.

They giggled.

"Problem solved," Rick said, raising his coffee to take a sip. He poured it down the front of his shirt.

"Shit," he said.

"You mean, shoot," Jeanne said.

"I didn't fasten the lid back on after I added milk."

Ella went and stood by Rick's side, as if in solidarity. "How did you know that's what they eat?"

"You look like twins," Jackson said.

"Alrighty then," Jeanne said, "now we need two changes of clothes."

Elves

It took them forty minutes to inch their way in line to the reception desk. Rick inquired if their room was ready, and was told by the desk clerk, a fifty-something-year-old man wearing a golden cardboard crown, that it was being sprinkled with magic dust. They'd have to wait another hour.

"Magic dust?" Rick said, looking at the desk clerk incredulously. "I think we can do without. We'll skip that part and take the room magic-free now."

"Dad!" the kids said, forever listening in. "We want the magic dust. We need it!"

"That's the whole point!" Jackson said. "Why do you think we came here in the first place?"

"It does help accelerate the journey from Apprentice to Master Wizard," the desk clerk said, a look of intense seriousness on his face. "It can happen twice as fast, sometimes quicker."

Jackson beamed.

"Fine, we'll just take our luggage for now," Jeanne said, giving him their ticket.

The desk clerk admired it as if it were a feather. "Enchanted," he said, bowing and disappearing through a glittery door. When he came out, his crown was noticeably shinier. He was empty-handed.

"It looks as though the elves have borrowed your luggage for a while," he said, smiling and sliding their ticket back.

The four of them blinked at him, the kids trying to decide if this was good news or bad.

"You mean our bags are lost?" Jeanne said.

Like the first desk clerk, this one had braces. Jeanne wondered if it was a promotion of some sort, then saw the poster-sized advertisement behind the front desk for Sweet Dreams Sedation Orthodontia. A princess was asleep on a thronelike dentist chair.

"Temporarily," the desk clerk said. "I'm sure they'll turn up. Sometimes there's a mix-up." He turned to the kids. "The good news is the elves tend to leave candy inside when they're done."

"Why do they need to borrow our suitcases?" Ella asked.

The desk clerk thought a moment. "They like to nap inside them."

"Oh," Ella said.

"They're picky," the desk clerk said. "They don't just take any old luggage. No siree."

"Did you actually look for our bags, or were you just back there polishing your crown?" Rick said.

The desk clerk looked confused.

"This is outrageous," Rick said.

"Oh, I don't know," the desk clerk said, winking at Ella and Jackson. His braces sparkled in the rotating ceiling light. "I'd say it's more than outrageous. I'd say it's outrageantastic. Because the elves provide one Great Enchanted Quest voucher for every child's suitcase they take. So I have two Great Enchanted Quest vouchers for you, at a value of over $150."

He rang a bell, and everyone around them cheered.

Great Enchanted Quest

Ella and Jackson ripped open the large sequined envelope containing the vouchers. "To the gift shop!" Jackson said, leading the way. He took Ella's hand and pulled her along. Jeanne had never seen him do that before. Ella skipped at his side, thrilled by the attention.

At the gift shop, the guy took the vouchers and inserted their wands into a machine that resembled a miniature MRI. It made a racket that sounded like a spoon banging a pan. The whole thing seemed fake to Jeanne—she'd had a real MRI before, for back pain—but the guy said, "Enjoy your quest." He gave Jackson and Ella each a booklet titled *The Ancient Book of Magic*.

"Dude!" Jackson said, wand in one hand, booklet in the other. "Now we're talking!" He held the booklet up to his face to read it—did he need glasses?—his bad arm bending out like an unfolded wing. Jeanne tried to decide if someone, say, an employer, would discriminate against Jackson, maybe not hire him. There were studies out there: being disfigured did not help with the job search. But Rick was always saying no one would notice unless they looked really closely, and who was going to do that? Who stared at other people's arms? Then again, Rick was also always trying to explain to Jeanne that money wasn't all it was cracked up to be. "You have the pony, but you're still miserable," he often said. Jeanne believed he had a reserve from childhood—memories of plenty—that provided him a cushion against the realities of life.

Jackson flipped to the first page of the booklet. "We need to find Bewitching Hall!" he said.

"I think there's a map by the elevator," Jeanne said.

The kids whooped down the hall, in the opposite direction of the elevator.

"Jeanne," Rick said, touching her arm in the doorway of the gift shop. He seemed short of breath. The coffee on his shirt was drying, giving the plaid a beige tinge. That was one of the nice things about the West Coast: it was forgiving. You could walk around with a large spill down your front, and no one would bat an eye.

"I know, you still haven't had your coffee," Jeanne said.

"I'm thinking I could be a CPA," he said. "I've been checking it out and there's a program where I could get an online degree in a year."

"An accountant?" Jeanne said.

"It sounds so clean, so cut and dry. I think I'm ready for something like that. No gray areas. Nothing lying around, gathering dust."

"Are you good with numbers?"

"I don't know. You're the one who always does our finances."

"I thought that was because you didn't like to."

"It was. But if someone's going to pay me a steady salary, if it's a nine-to-five job benefiting my family, I think I'd feel different. With the additional income, we could start hiring a babysitter every once in a while, get a break. Maybe think about moving to a better school district."

"Are you sure?"

The kids came swooping back, cawing like crows, Jackson cradling his defective arm because it tired easily. Rick and Jeanne had been told that physical therapy might help.

Rick glanced at the arm. "I'm positive."

Ella rammed her head into Jeanne's thigh.

"Ella," Jeanne said, "you can't do that to Mommy. It hurts and it gives me bruises."

Ella turned and stabbed Rick in the side of the leg with her wand, piercing an old ACL injury left over from Rick's varsity soccer days.

"Ow! All right, let's go." Rick rubbed his knee.

"There's a map by the elevator," Jeanne repeated. "It's the other way down the hall."

The kids went the other way down the hall, zigzagging back and forth, bouncing off walls, flinging themselves from one side to the other. When a heavyset man eating a billow of cotton candy appeared, they almost knocked him over.

"How many hours do we have left in this hellhole?" Rick said.

"Forty-six," Jeanne said.

Rick rolled his eyes and jogged off.

Jeanne stepped out of the gift shop and stood in the hall, watching her husband lumber after the kids. When they met in Bali, he was lanky. She'd weighed more than him at the time; the joke was, in the ocean, she'd been the one to cradle him in her arms. But now, well, he was barrel-chested. She'd need a forklift. That was middle age for you. It was ruthless.

The kids went around a corner. Her husband followed. Jeanne strolled down the hall, buying herself a few minutes of alone-time. The doors to the rooms were metallic with jewel-studded numbers. Various ornate plaques hung above them: Wizard's Roost, Pixie's Place, Dragon's Lair. Through one open door, she saw a family of four in a suite, jean-clad parents with Venti coffees, and a pair of twins—three, maybe four years old—nursing Disney sippy cups. They lounged together on a king-size bed, zoned out in front of the TV. It occurred to Jeanne that after Rick got a serious job, they would be able to afford vacations. They could stay at decent hotels and get adjoining rooms, tell the kids not to bother them before 7 a.m. They could eat Clif Bars, maybe get a house with a yard. A yard would make a difference, especially for Ella. And a good school, of course.

A sense of relief washed over Jeanne. Maybe she and Rick had made some mistakes, gone on too long in search of their individual ideals. Maybe they'd made some bad judgment calls, not knowing when to call it quits in the name of art or Bali or whatever. But they were free to start over. Yes, Jackson had the arm issue, but it could be worse. No one had leukemia. No one was breathing through a ventilator. Yes, there would be heartbreak, but they could adapt. She thought of the way her captive cardinalfish specimens in Bali adjusted to diurnal living.

Jeanne moved out of the doorway of the suite when one of the twins waved at her. She must have been staring.

She continued down the hall and turned the corner. There, she witnessed Rick holding Ella's wand over his head with one hand while ripping Jackson's away with the other. Rick marched over to a chrome trash bin and stuffed them inside. Ella yowled. Jackson threw himself down on the floor.

"What happened?" Jeanne said.

"Time-out!" Rick said. "We're taking a family time-out! We'll meet back here in ten minutes!"

Then Rick fell to his knees facing the trash bin. In the warped reflection of the chrome, Jeanne saw his tongue flick out. His eyes rolled back into his head. He rocked forward onto his hands, then pushed himself up to standing.

"What was that?" Jeanne said. "Did you just faint?"

"Probably from lack of coffee," Rick said.

He opened the nearest door—a heavy gray one with a do-not-enter sticker that led to some kind of humming electrical room—and slipped inside. The door clicked shut behind him.

Jeanne fished through the trash and handed the wands back to her sobbing kids. Jackson accepted his lying on the floor. The sobs subsided into hiccups. Families entered and exited the elevator, wielding wands and lollipops and pinwheels. They stepped over Jackson. A hyperactive girl in a tutu brazenly tapped him with her wand. Because the rules of the family time-out dictated each family member be alone, Jeanne went through another door, and enclosed herself in a supply closet filled with mini soaps and shampoos. She thought she caught a whiff of cocamide DEA, a carcinogen commonly found in bath products. She couldn't stop picturing the whites of Rick's eyes.

She and Rick, the kids, they were all doomed.

In her wallet, she found a business card—the flimsy kind you could get for free on the Internet—for Bob's Coffee. It didn't even have a logo, not even a steaming cup. Jackson could have done a better job designing it.

She dialed the number and Bob himself answered the phone. She'd met him once before, a guy in a smashed-up cowboy hat.

"I'd like to buy the masks," she said.

"Say what?"

"The masks you're displaying on your walls. I'd like to buy them."

"Which one?"

"All of them."

"All ten?"

"That's right."

She agreed to pay for the packaging and shipping. She gave him her credit card number and address. Reluctantly, she gave him her name.

"Wait, aren't you his—?"

"I'd like to remain anonymous."

"No further questions," he said.

Ten minutes later, back at the elevator, Rick seemed fine. She searched for signs: no paleness, no shallow breath. He could walk without shuffling his feet. When she asked him what day it was, he looked at her strangely but answered correctly. The kids were standing, clutching wands to chests.

"Now where were we headed again?" Rick said.

"Bewitching Hall," Jackson said. "It says in the *The Ancient Book of Magic* we're supposed to take the stairs to make questing easier and faster."

"What floor is it on?" Rick said.

Jackson looked at the map on the wall. "Fifth."

"That'll be the elevator for us," Rick said.

The elevator arrived empty, smelling of caramel corn. They all got on. Jackson let Ella press the button for the fifth floor, another first. The elevator went up, screeched, then jerked to a halt.

"Are we there yet?" Ella said. The vomit on her jumpsuit had hardened into petal-like clumps, Hello Kitty in a swirl of crusty off-color leaves.

Rick tried to peer through the crack between the elevator doors. "I think we're about five feet from the second floor."

"Ella, sweetie," Jeanne said. "Could you press that red button right there."

"The one with the E?"

"Yes, that one."

Ella pressed it with the tip of her wand.

"Does this mean we're stuck?" Jackson said.

"Yup," Rick said, sliding his back down the wall.

In the distance, there was the sound of an alarm bell. Rick sat probing his knee. Ella wanted Jeanne to pick her up. Jeanne plopped down across from Rick and held Ella in her lap. Something sticky snagged at Jeanne's pants. There was a smaller, closer bell ringing over the alarm bell. Rick looked at his phone.

"Oh, Jesus, it's Bob again. He probably wants me to cut my heart out and serve it to him on a platter."

"You should answer it," Jeanne said.

"I guess I can be an adult."

Rick closed his eyes, managed a "hello" into the phone. There was a short pause before his eyes opened. He turned his back on Jeanne, mumbled a few okays, a thanks, and hung up. He didn't move. He ran his hand over his face.

"What did he say?" Jeanne said.

"Nothing."

"He must have said something."

"He wants to wish me luck in my future endeavors."

"That's it?"

"He's not exactly the chatty type." Rick slipped the phone back into his jeans pocket.

They heard voices above. The elevator doors opened to a concrete wall, on which stood the shoes and shins of several Enchanted Inn staff.

"Have I got a surprise for you, buddy," one of them said, lowering himself down onto his stomach to talk to Jackson.

"For me?" Jackson said, as if no one had paid attention to him his whole life.

The guy peered in. "I heard a rumor there are two Master Wizards in here. A brother and sister to be exact."

Jeanne recognized him. He was the guy from the gift shop. He emptied a bag of plastic runes and medallions and crystals onto the second floor, lining them up, making a trail leading away from the elevator, as if that were the only way to convince them to climb out.

The power had gone out during the night, and my fan stood motionless, soft, gray dust like fur on its blades. The beads hanging down in the doorway to my toilet were still. If you watched carefully enough, you could see air rising off the warped linoleum floor.

"Hot enough for you?" Derrick said.

I felt my forehead. "This would be considered a fever in the States."

We lay on our backs and blinked up at the water-damaged ceiling, at the cracks that—after ten months of staring at them—reminded me of tectonic plates, something I'd studied in a class I failed at a school I no longer attended.

It was the cheapest room I could find, my first place away from home.

"Got a cigarette for an old man?" Derrick said, sitting up and coughing. The room smelled like baked concrete. "I'm out."

I fished around for my pack, found it flattened at our feet.

"That settles it." He rocked his body back and forth, gathering momentum to stand. After spending the night on my tatami, you could feel gravity sucking your bones to the floor.

He pulled on a pair of khaki shorts, hopping on one foot. He found his shirt on a peg over the toilet. "Be right back."

Ten minutes later, he returned carrying a small battery-powered fan and two packs of Longlifes. He moved the mosquito coil, set the fan down in its place, and kicked off his clothes. We took turns nursing the breeze. He faced away to light us cigarettes. It was Sunday, our one day off from teaching ESL.

"What?" I said, because he kept getting up to glance out the window, trying to angle himself so he could see out front. I could have told him without looking there was a pack of hairless dogs and an abandoned food cart missing its wheels below.

"There's a guy with red hair out there. First one I've seen in Tainan."

"Down below?"

"In front of the building. Can't see him from here."

"Red hair? He's screwed."

"Looks completely lost."

"What's he doing?"

"Standing in front of the building like it's a bus stop or something. Attracting a crowd."

"He's just standing there?"

"I think he has a bloody nose. He's pinching his nostrils and tilting his head back. It's stuff like this that makes foreigners look bad."

"Did he say anything?"

"Nope."

"What's he wearing?"

"I don't know. Pants. A large fanny pack that's shouting, 'Rob me!'"

"How old is he?"

"Fifties."

I pulled my hair into a ponytail. "I've got to check this out."

I threw on a skirt and went downstairs. Outside, the air was hazy, the traffic beginning to wake up. The man was rifling through a cheap leather bag with a strap that made it look like an overstuffed woman's purse. A small crowd had stopped—five, six people on scooters—pointing and marveling.

I walked up and stood behind him. He was still searching through his bag, peering inside, the hair on his neck slick with sweat. Finally, he pulled out a cotton ball. The bystanders seemed let down; a few of them lowered their face shields over their helmets and drove off. One of them honked his horn long and hard, as if to say, Get this show on the road. The red-haired man was completely oblivious, as only one person I knew could be.

"Lee," I said. "What are you doing here?"

He stuffed the cotton ball up his nostril and turned around. There was a little blood, not much. "Blair. What am I doing here?"

Already, I was annoyed. Here was a man incapable of surprise. He had a way of repeating everything you said in a voice that made every situation seem mundane. The first time he spent the night at our house, not even a year after my father died, this is how he calmed my mother down after she woke up from one of her nightmares, pleading with the dead body of my father in her sleep. I was used to bringing her tall glasses of ginger ale and gin—G&Gs we called them, and sometimes we would sit in her bed and share one—but that night I stood in the doorway while he held her head in his hands and said, "It's okay to let him go. Now's as good a time as any."

Soon after, my mother stopped having nightmares. Cure by boredom.

"We tried calling, writing," he said. "We couldn't get through. So I came here to find you."

"Why didn't she come herself?"

He nodded, as if to indicate I'd asked a good question. Before he worked with therapy horses, leading emotionally disturbed children on ponies around rings, he taught fifth grade for twenty years, and this was one of his remaining tics. "We thought about it long and hard. We thought it would be best if it was just me. Your mother, you know, it's best for her to remain calm."

"So she stayed home?"

"She stayed home." He unplugged his nostril and examined the cotton ball. The bleeding had stopped. "She misses you."

"Please."

"She does."

"Well, you can tell her you found me."

"Or, was it the other way around?" He was smiling, but there were red splotches gathering like storm clouds on his neck. His face looked freshly sunburnt, the color of a peach. He had the kind of skin that flushes and pales according to weather or mood.

Two more scooters took off, and two others landed, the drivers walking them in so that the front fenders were inches from Lee's shins. It was a swarm of handlebars and wheels.

"Are there any traffic rules here?" he said.

"You should see Taipei."

"And the pollution."

"It grows on you."

"The noise. I can't hear myself think."

"What'd you say?"

He was wearing a crumpled linen shirt that was splattered with mud, as though someone had driven through a puddle and splashed him, but there hadn't been rain for weeks. That was Lee for you: inexplicable splotches and stains, as if everywhere he went people jumped out from nowhere and dumped things over his head.

I used to shout, *"Lee*ave me alone, Lee," after he and my mom were married, when he would try to help me with my homework, angling my desk lamp over my notebook so I wasn't reading in the dark.

He'd hold his hands up in the air and say, "Okey dokey. Backing off." He never had kids of his own.

A tap on my shoulder made me jump. It was Derrick, hastily dressed, his shirt buttoned halfway. "Everything all right?"

"Derrick, this is my stepfather, Lee."

Derrick stretched out a hand. "Nice to meet you."

"Likewise." Lee's eyes darted over Derrick's open shirt, his pale, hairless chest, his state of disarray, having come from the same door I did, which could only mean one thing.

Lee was staying at the Oriental Hotel, near the train station, and we arranged that I would meet him there that night after he woke up. He was in Taiwan for four days—one of which was almost over—and planned to stay on American time. I found him in the lobby, standing, reading *Gulliver's Travels,* hardback, checked out from the New Canaan Library and lugged all the way here. In his other hand, he held what looked like a squashed Fig Newton wrapped in paper towel. Sometimes I wondered if my mother married him because nothing about him could ever possibly remind her of my father. My father was known for beating the stock market, serving in tennis before his opponent was ready, and smoking Cuban cigars. Lee had smoked a cigarette once, he told me, but never inhaled.

The hotel was a dump—even for thrifty Lee—the carpets worn, the windows filmy, the walls discolored in a way that made you think of peeling skin. The furniture was institutional, dirty browns and oranges good at masking stains. You could hear buses going by, the traffic stalling and congesting outside. It was in a part of town foreigners called the Dead Zone, where it was rumored the traffic exhaust made birds drop out of the sky. You could take a detour, turning left after the Bank of Taiwan and jogging around the Great South Gate, but I'd come to like the fumes, like a kid inhaling the smell of gasoline.

There was a desk clerk and a bellhop in polyester tunics, who welcomed and ushered me through the door, but soon after turned their attention back to Lee. They were watching his hair closely, as if they thought it might try to escape. Lee paced the lobby, playing the part. One thing he was good at: reading while walking. He liked to say his preferred mode of travel was books.

"How'd you find this place?" I said.

He lowered his book and slipped his finger inside to mark his page. There were crumbs on his lips but I tried not to let them get to me. "There was a little confusion. I was supposed to be staying at another Oriental Hotel, at the other end of town. Actually, it appears there are three Oriental Hotels. Maybe more." He had the dry, red-rimmed eyes of someone who'd been tossing and turning in an unfamiliar bed.

"Want to move somewhere else?"

He did, but I knew he wouldn't. He wouldn't send a hamburger back in a restaurant if he were served Spam on toast.

"No, no. I'm quite all right."

Normally, I might have asked the desk clerk and the bellhop what they were looking at, but it was nice to have the attention drawn away from me, my blond, frizzy hair.

"I'm starving," Lee said. "What do people eat around here?"

I shrugged my shoulders. "Food."

There was Macanna Beer House, and an expensive place called The Ambassador, and the onion cakes on Shengli Road, and, of course, hundreds of noodle and fried rice stands, dumpling restaurants, vegetarian buffets—standard places you took visiting friends or relatives to ease them into things, but I led Lee to a gold-toothed woman selling rubbery brown cuts of meat: pig knuckles, innards, chicken necks and feet. Lee looked down at his choices then up at me, with schoolteacher patience. You had to give him credit: I'd been in Taiwan for ten months and I could barely look at the stuff.

"They have beer here?" he said.

"Sure."

I ordered and we sat down at a small table on the side of the street. I could feel the sweat on my face evaporate into the night air.

"You speak Chinese," he said.

"I get by."

I nibbled a piece of skin off a chicken claw and swigged down half a can of Taiwan Beer. Lee watched me and did the same. People flocked to the tables around us, ordering nothing, gawking at Lee like teenagers in love.

"What are those? Gizzards?" he said, suddenly standing up and looking back through the plastic window at the assortment of meats. I noticed miniature tongues—chicken? duck?—for the first time. The woman was watching a variety show on a television attached to a wall, the audience clapping and going wild.

"I don't know. We'll find out."

I ordered a small plate of them. The woman brought them over with chopsticks. Lee held one in each hand, then gave up and ate with his fingers.

"Gizzards," he said.

"Really?"

"Try one, they're good."

"That's okay, I'll stick to chicken feet."

"More for me."

I ordered two more beers. Lee chewed slowly, made his way through half of what was on his plate. I pretended not to be hungry.

"Am I imagining things or is everybody looking at me?"

"They've never seen red hair."

"Ah."

A man across the way stepped out of a barbershop and tossed a bucket of water into the street. A woman drove by on a scooter balancing a birdcage in her lap. You could see the flickering lights of a karaoke bar through a second-story window, the shadow of someone dancing alone. Two stalls over, someone was serving beef noodles—my mouth watered at the smell—but luckily Lee was facing the other way. We were sitting on small stools and my legs were going numb.

"So I came with good news," he said.

Divorce, I immediately thought, but then realized that would be good news only to me.

"Oh?" I shifted my weight, felt the blood rush into my calves.

"But your mother wants to be the one to tell it."

"She's here?"

"No, but I told her we'd call at midnight. Eleven in the morning her time."

"In an hour?"

The people around us were listening intently now, leaning forward in their seats, but it was hard to tell how much they understood. One man had left and returned with a lawn chair.

Lee looked at them, at me, then down at his plastic digital watch, as if we were all in this together. "Exactly right."

At 11:30 p.m., we climbed the stairs to the third floor of his hotel—the elevator was out of order—and by 11:40, we were sitting in his room, Lee on the end of a twin bed with a shiny polyester cover that looked wet, me in an uncomfortable metal chair. It was like cheap hotel rooms everywhere: smoke-stained walls, an abundance of frazzled hairs, the feeling that if you tossed a lit match the whole thing would go up in flames. And like people in cheap hotel rooms everywhere, Lee kept looking at his watch.

"Twenty minutes to go," he said.

"I'm ready."

"I asked for nonsmoking," he said, scratching his neck. It looked like he'd been clawed by a bear.

"No such thing here."

He opened a guidebook to confirm the international prefix and the country code, and had me write down the number we were going to dial on a pad of Post-its he'd brought from the States. I read it out loud.

"Are you sure you start with 002?" he said.

"Positive."

"Two zeros?"

"Right."

"Do you wait after that, or dial the whole thing all at once."

"You dial it all at once."

"I haven't talked with your mother for over thirty-six hours. I don't want to screw this up." He stood up from the bed and sat back down.

"I understand. I haven't spoken to her in ten months."

You could always tell when Lee had been drinking because his cheeks turned rosy like a doll's and his lips hung there, sluggish and loose, as if they couldn't muster up the energy to formulate a word. His face gave everything away, and he always claimed that's what kept him honest.

He was looking around the room now, tapping his foot. He always wore loafers with tassels, and once when I was fifteen I cut them off because they drove me up the wall. He didn't get angry, just walked around in his shoes with their nubs, but my mother—and this was the only time—pulled me into the bathroom and slapped me. My father, had it been him, would have congratulated me on the joke and changed into one of his twenty other pairs.

"Don't tell her we've been drinking," Lee said, exhaling into his hand and smelling his breath.

"I won't."

"She's on an anti-alcohol kick. We both were."

"We'll say the connection's bad."

Lee pushed off his loafers and tucked his feet under himself on the bed. I tilted my head over the back of the chair.

At 11:50, the room silent, I looked around.

"Lee," I said. "Where's the phone?"

He unwound his legs, shoved his loafers back on. "Darn it!"

We sprinted down the three flights of stairs to the lobby, where the desk clerk and the bellhop were flicking small wads of crumpled paper off the reception counter onto the floor. When they looked up to see Lee, one of them blurted out, "Redhead," in English, as if surprised to encounter a species known to be extinct. I asked them in Chinese about the phones, and they informed me there were none in the rooms. They instructed us to use the communal one behind the stairs.

I pulled Lee down a dark hallway to a small nook with a phone and a stool—four minutes to go—where it became apparent Lee's calling card wasn't going to work. I told him to stay there and ran back out to the desk clerk and bellboy, who directed me to a 7-Eleven on the other side of the train station to buy a telephone card.

It was one in the morning by the time we got through. Lee dialed the number himself and closed his eyes and jumped off the stool when she answered: "Thank God!" I could hear my mom's voice. She said she'd been calling another Oriental Hotel, one where they did have phones in the rooms. Lee explained the mix-up, and I heard her ask him if he was okay. He was hanging in there, he said, but most importantly he'd found me. My mom sounded pleased. Then she went on to tell him about how she'd used the new spray nozzle on the hose to water the hydrangeas in back—a marriage of passion—before Lee turned over the phone.

"Hi, Mom."

"Blair."

"Mom?"

"I knew you wouldn't let me down."

"Can you hear me?"

The line beeped and there was static and then it went dead. I shook the receiver and slapped it against the palm of my hand, then gave it to Lee, who did the same. I ran out to get help. The desk clerk followed me back and told me my card had run out of time. I looked at Lee and he said, "Fly like the wind!" So I ran out into the night again, through a stream of scooters, over construction debris, past an assortment of gelatinous duck eggs set out on small white plates, and returned with three more cards.

At two in the morning, I read out the number and Lee dialed again.

No answer.

"What day is it? What day is it?" Lee shouted, putting his ear to the receiver one last time before hanging up.

"Monday for us. Sunday for her."

"Oh, God, she has that damn riding session. I arranged it. Stupid!"

"It's okay, Lee. We'll call another time."

He leaned forward, tipped his face into his hands. "All I can do is try my best, right? All I can do is try."

I thought some food would help to sober us up, rein the melodrama in. "You hungry?" I said.

Lee didn't answer, instead looked across the hall like I'd insulted him but he was too principled to fight back.

"I know a good noodle place."

"Noodles?" he said. "As in spaghetti?"

My stomach growled but Lee didn't give a sign if he heard. "You can get them in a soup or dry."

"Without intestines?"

"Any way you like. Vegetarian, if you want."

He stood up. "Lead the way."

We went to an all-night noodle place, the one two stalls over from the chicken feet stand, and sat in plastic chairs in a corner, at a table the size of a tray. I held my noodle bowl in my hand so Lee could set his down. Around us, university students with uniform black bangs crammed for exams.

"She sound happy?" he said.

"Yeah, what's the deal?"

"Say she was proud?"

"I think she's the one who's drunk."

"Blair," Lee said. "You've been accepted to Wescott Academy."

I was holding a piece of fishcake between my chopsticks and I dropped it back into my soup.

"Do they know about me getting kicked out?"

"They know all of that."

"What did you do? Pay them off?"

"As if we had that kind of money."

He was looking at me with that intense gaze of his, the one that made you feel like he had high expectations of you, and that if he came on too strong sometimes, it was because you were the best student in his class.

"Well, I guess I'm surprised," I said.

"Don't answer one way or the other now. Just think about it. Let the idea settle in."

I tried to picture myself lining up in yet another dining hall, or sneaking a cigarette in a new dorm, or signing out to go to a Friendly's or Denny's in the nearest excuse for a town, but it all seemed completely removed from where I was, sitting in a noodle stall, fly strips hanging down like streamers from above, ten feet from a scabby gutter dog licking a sore on its leg. I had vague recollection of a blue exam booklet in which I wrote an essay on a book I never read.

"They didn't need an essay, a personal statement?" I said.

"Funny you should ask."

"I didn't even have to fill out an application."

He rubbed his lips with his fingers and closed his eyes. "The truth of the matter is I wanted to come here alone so I could tell you that I did."

"Did what?"

"I applied for you."

"You mean, like, in my name?"

Lee nodded, looked down. I pushed back my chair. I finally had a reason to be angry at him—it was the first thing he'd done wrong in the three years I'd known him—but all I could do was laugh.

"It wasn't a high point in my life," he said. "I didn't think it through."

I grabbed his hand across the table and shook it. "Way to go, Lee!"

"I knew how much it would mean to your mother and I got carried away."

"They couldn't tell it wasn't me?"

"I apologize."

"I'm proud of you, Lee!"

"It was wrong."

He looked down into his noodle bowl, as if to double-check its contents, make sure a stray organ hadn't slipped in. He'd had trouble with the chopsticks and they lay splayed across the rim of his bowl. He'd tried to make do with a plastic soupspoon but the noodles kept sliding off.

"Cheer up, Lee," I said. "You're a rebel now."

I ordered us two tall bottles of beer, three times the size of what we'd been drinking before. They came out lukewarm, but I was used to it and I knew Lee wouldn't complain. He sighed and slugged a quarter of the thing down.

"So what did you write about?" I said. "My first menstruation?"

Lee shook his head, took another swig. His cheeks were regaining their rosy glow.

"What, then?"

"Oh, the usual personal-statement-type things. You've seen one, you've seen them all."

I imagined the admissions committee—a panel of dark-suited men and the one token woman, maybe the chaplain's wife—reading it, eyes glazing over. Lee said he quit teaching because he wasn't getting enough support from the administration, but I always pictured him looking up from the blackboard to find his entire class asleep.

"How many pages?"

"Seven."

"Single-spaced or double?"

"Single."

"No word limit?"

"I went way over it. They didn't seem to mind."

"I would never have guessed you had it in you."

"I'm just, I'm not sure how to proceed from here." He pressed his hand over his mouth.

"You know what would be great?" I said. "If you could take the SATs for me too." I clicked my beer bottle against his, splashing the contents, nearly knocking his out of his hand.

"Seriously," I said, "what was it about? In case someone asks me, I should know."

"Oh, the regular bull, growing up. The kinds of things admissions folks like to hear."

"That's good, Lee. That's good. Did you mention my father?"

"Uh-huh, yes."

"What was the first sentence?"

He paused. "Let me think." He looked askance at the spattered wall beside us, did a double take, as if seeing a reflection of himself.

"Come on, Lee. What was the first sentence?"

He set down his beer.

"Tell me."

"'I was fourteen years old when my father committed suicide.'"

The proprietor of the noodle stall, a friendly man with girl-thin arms, was standing over us, asking where we were from. I said America, and he wanted to know the color of Lee's hair. I told him red, and watched him make calculations in his head, reassessing what was possible and what was not. He pulled out a cigarette, as if to help him absorb the shock. I asked him for one, and he lit it for me before turning back to take an order.

"You're fucking kidding me, Lee. What'd you do, write about me going into the garage and finding him there?"

Lee nodded, holding his beer bottle in front of his face like a shield.

"And the blood on the car I thought was mud?"

"I didn't think any other essay would get you in."

"Mom let you write it?"

"She doesn't know."

"How could she not know?"

"She thinks you sent it in."

"From Taiwan?"

"That's why she's so proud."

"You lied to her?"

"Just this once. I've never seen her want anything so bad."

"So you lied." I exhaled smoke over the table at him, but he didn't try to wave it off.

He took another swig of beer, held it in his mouth, swallowed.

"What you're doing," he said, "getting kicked out of school after school, moving eight thousand miles away from home, having relations with someone twice your age—I'm not blind—all this time I thought it was about your father."

"Well, you wrote the essay. You should know."

"Then I realized it's about me."

"Because you're so important in my life?"

"Before me, you were all she had. There were nights you slept in the same bed."

"She told you that?"

"Then I came along."

I was going to ditch him there—what better place than a noodle stall in a foreign city on a street with a thousand Chinese signs? A taxi had pulled up and parked against a table, and the driver, drunk, was spitting betelnut juice, red like blood, on the ground. The proprietor didn't like it, and I could tell there was going to be a fight. A small crowd was gathering and I knew it wouldn't be long before they fixed their gaze on Lee.

But when I stood up to leave, Lee jumped up too, and I figured his smoky dump of a room was punishment enough. I walked out, and he followed behind, saying, "If I could do it over, Blair, I would. I mean it. I would." We left the crowd and walked down streets that were empty except for gutter dogs humping and wailing into the night. In an alley, a rusty motorcycle lay on its side, stripped of parts. I heard the cough of a scooter that wouldn't start. The alcohol was beginning to wear off, and I could feel a headache coming on.

At the door of the Oriental Hotel, I stopped. Lee didn't know where we were until I pointed it out.

"I'm leaving tomorrow," he said. "Changed my flight. I need my Shredded Wheat. I need to get back where I belong."

He pulled an envelope from his pocket and held it out to me. For a second, I thought he was trying to buy my mother off me with cash to even things out.

"It's a ticket," he said. "Come back and get a summer job, earn some money before classes start."

"No, thanks."

He put it in my hand. "In case you change your mind."

"I won't."

"What's the name of your Chinese friend?"

"Derrick. He's American."

"Please say goodbye to him for me."

Behind him, through the glass door of the lobby, I could see the desk clerk and the bellhop goofing off, playing some game in which they each had five seconds to mess up the other's hair. Lee turned to clasp the handle of the door, then turned back.

"I want you to know I'm going to come clean to your mother."

"Lee," I said. "Don't."

"It's the right thing to do."

"You'll only upset her. You know how she is. It will be hard enough on her when you tell her I'm not going back to school."

He opened the door, held it with his foot for a moment, then went inside. The desk clerk and the bellhop stood up and welcomed him with exaggerated smiles. As soon as he passed the broken elevator and disappeared up the stairs, they took turns imitating him, stumbling dejectedly across the lobby, blinking and sniffling, until I finally banged on the glass and asked them to stop.

1.

We had agreed to meet at the Happy Life Guesthouse in Bangkok, and Jack was the first to arrive, looking like he'd stepped out of an REI catalog, then me, Paula, Adam, Stever, and JC. Paula hiked and hitchhiked the whole way there, of course, adamant about making the trip as challenging as possible. Adam and Stever randomly ran into each other in a pagoda in Vietnam a month after our trek in Nepal—a testament to the incestuousness of the traveling circuit—then parted ways again. JC went to see some girl in Singapore who turned out not to be there anymore. I rode trains across China looking for good material for a magazine article, but ended up writing sappy, pathetic journal entries on how at the age of twenty-four I was forever destined to be alone.

Two minutes passed and we were at it again, Adam annoying the rest of us by cracking sunflower seeds between his teeth, shells splitting and falling and some actually flinging out among us.

"Why can't you eat something normal like an apple?" Stever said.

We got a dorm room together and the first thing Adam did was stand on one of the rickety cots to see if he could look over into the next room. The walls were as thin as cardboard, with nothing but chicken wire up top. He'd just pulled himself up, squinting with exertion, when I heard the guy in that room telling him to fuck off.

"Take it easy, chief," Adam said, holding his hand up in peace and climbing back down.

Paula tested the cots and chose the hardest mattress, which was about two inches thick and had stains in the shape of clouds. She didn't want to spoil herself with a soft one because it would make it difficult to go back to sleeping on the ground. I took out some ginger candy I'd bought in Chengdu and passed it around. JC sniffed it before he put it in his mouth. Stever was off to the sinks, probably searching for a mirror. He'd been on a remote island off of Thailand and hadn't been able to look at himself for a total of eight days.

"That's weird Kippy didn't show," JC said, unraveling two carved wooden pipes from a red bandana. The first thing he said when he met me was, "I love drugs." He had a small goatee that made it look like something was perpetually dripping from his chin. He'd been living on eight dollars a day, and was the only one who'd been traveling for longer than me, about three years.

"Probably just delayed is all," Adam said, watching JC inspect a ball of hash. "You know how transportation is."

"Maybe he forgot about us," Jack said. "A lot can happen in two months." He chucked tickets, receipts, and coins into piles on his cot, taking inventory. The pockets of his shorts hung inside out like tongues.

"That *is* weird," I said. "Wasn't it his idea to meet up in the first place?"

"Come on, Rachel," Stever said to me, back from the sinks, hair slicked behind his ears. "Don't take it so hard. I'm here."

"It's not only me," I said, and everyone nodded. "You'd think he'd be the first to arrive."

Well, it turned out he did come, only he was two days late.

2.

The Happy Life Guesthouse was a faded-blue, four-story building, riddled with pockmarks where pieces of concrete had fallen out. There were eight windowless rooms on each floor, and sinks and showers at the end of each hall near the stairs. Inside the entrance, there was a simple café with a bunch of white plastic tables and chairs where you could sit and people-watch. The building was set off from the main street, on one of the few alleys where it was possible to step outside the front door and not get immediately run over. There was a man with a floppy eyelid selling pineapple on thin wooden sticks across the way, and a lopsided noodle stall that always seemed deserted. A pack of mangy dogs flitted around like minnows on a never-ending search for food.

We were playing cards in the café downstairs, drinking Singha beers and filtered water, when Kippy stumbled through the open door of the guesthouse, tripping over someone's backpack and hanging on to the corner of a table for support. The couple (Swedish, I think) sitting there looked at him through overgrown bangs, displeased. We were near the front desk, surrounded by twenty or so grungy travelers. There was an eleven-year-old boy taking orders on a small pad and passing them through a window in back of the room. He had a Walkman clipped to the waist of his Levi's, and while he waited for the food to come out, he pressed the earphones against one ear and swayed his head from side to side.

Stever was smiling because he'd gotten a royal flush. We were gambling with baht (we let Paula use the rest of her rupees too) and he was winning. Stever was cocky and he had a right to be. Not only did he always win, but he was gorgeous. Before we met him, he had a two-year modeling stint in Japan. "You just want to fuck me and you know it," he liked to say to men and women alike who gave him a hard time. The rest of us would go into convulsions, of course, pretending to barf.

"When he comes over, let's pretend we're asleep," Adam said. Adam performed improv in college and had us doing stuff like this all the time, as if we were his new troupe. He'd been traveling for almost a year, since the day after he graduated.

We watched Kippy out of the corners of our eyes. He let go of the table and steadied himself, knees bent and one foot in front of the other, the way you'd walk across a balance beam. He had a green tent bag tied to his wrist, which was strange, because before, he'd worn an old-school knapsack with leather straps that everyone, even passersby, admired. He crossed the room and stared down into someone's water glass, maybe trying to catch his reflection or see if there was something in his eye. His cheeks were gaunt, like he was sucking them in, and his collarbone jutted out like a shelf beneath his shirt. He was wearing a pair of baggy gray sweatpants that belonged to someone three sizes larger.

He slid down into the nearest chair (white, plastic like the rest). His eyes darted around the room, and I tried to see what he saw. First, he looked at the eleven-year-old boy and laughed lightly (at his Levi's, which were ripped at the knees, or the snapping of his fingers, which was now being joined by a hip-swiveling walk and slowly turning into a dance?). The boy used the words "Not possible" whenever the kitchen had run out of something you ordered. He was saying "Not possible" to two women in oversized sunglasses who nodded gravely and reluctantly picked something else.

There were little scenes, actions, and words floating around the tables, dangling in midair as though held there by string. A man sitting on the floor in the corner was playing the harmonica, a tune that made you feel you were lying in a gutter somewhere, down on your luck. The two women in oversized sunglasses were absorbed in a game of cat's cradle, transferring an intricately looped piece of yarn back and forth between outstretched hands. If there was someone smiling at one end of the room, there was someone weeping at the other. I couldn't blame Kippy for looking around.

But he was dirty, dirtier than I remembered him being on the trek, where bucket-baths were few and far between. His hair was matted and dusty, a rug that needed to be shaken out. His lips were cracked, fried from the sun, but the rest of him was an incandescent white. He was missing a tooth, and I didn't remember him missing one before. It was one of the side teeth you could see only when he smiled. Kippy was smiling, but not at us. He was looking up and around, as if following the arc of a rainbow.

"Yo, Kippy!" someone finally said, I think Paula. "We're over here." She had the husky voice of someone who'd partied all night, which wasn't far from the truth.

Kippy blinked and bucked as if a bird had swooped down right in front of his face.

"Good God," the woman at the next table over said, dropping her fork. Her boyfriend took her wrist.

That's when we got the sense something was wrong.

3.

Here are the things we knew about Kippy: That first day on the trek, the day the bus dropped us off at the edge of the trail and we became a group of travelers hiking in the same direction, Jack remembered him squatting down to examine the gnarled root of a tree that was growing up instead of down. He borrowed Jack's travel knife to scrape the surface of a fungus resembling a seashell. He tasted things—random petals and berries—and carried a book on plants so he could look up the names. He loved rhododendrons. In the evenings, at dinner, when the rest of us rubbed Jack's Bengay on aching muscles and complained about having to eat fried potatoes every night, Kippy had a look of anticipation on his face, as if he thought one of us might suddenly reveal we were royalty traveling in disguise. One night, when we went around the table and talked about what we dreamed of (being rich, being famous), Jack remembered Kippy saying, "You guys have it all wrong. This is the shit, man. Right here."

We all agreed he was solid, down-to-earth. ("Not like you, Stever," Paula managed to squeeze in.) He seemed to be traveling for all the right reasons—to learn more about the world, see what he was missing. He'd had some shitty factory job in the States on and off for five years, working on an assembly line, putting rubber stoppers in bottles. ("Fascinating!" I remember Stever saying to him. "Oh tell us more! Tell us more!") He was the only one of us who hadn't gone to college, but he'd educated himself by reading newspapers and anything he could get his hands on, and Jack, who had a master's degree in biology and was planning on getting a Ph.D., thought he was smart.

Adam remembered Kippy telling him late one night that the challenges you faced traveling were indelibly imprinted on your soul.

"You mean like the time I shat my pants on that thirty-six-hour bus-ride to Tibet and everyone knew from the smell and moved to the opposite end of the bus?" Adam said to him then.

Kippy didn't miss a beat. "Exactly what I'm talking about."

The day we walked through the swamp and got covered in leeches, when all of us were going crazy burning them off with cigarettes and roaches because the owner of the guesthouse had run out of salt, JC saw Kippy petting a leech on his ankle.

"Maybe I was really fucked up," JC said, "but he just whistled to himself softly while the thing grew to the size of a golf ball."

He was double-jointed. On one of the early days of the trek he ended up falling into step with Stever. ("Of all people!" Paula said.

"It's a wonder he didn't hightail it home.") Stever wasn't sure why, maybe as an icebreaker, but Kippy stopped and showed him how he could put his legs around his head.

"He sat there in the path and twisted himself up like a deformed beggar," Stever said. "I think he was taking the piss out of me."

"Or else," Paula said, "he was sick and tired of hearing you talk about yourself."

Stever smiled one of his you-want-me smiles.

Paula knew that when Kippy'd had a few drinks, he had trouble getting it up. "Or maybe it was the weed," she said. Along one section of the path there were stalks and stalks.

"Okay, thanks for the useful information," the rest of us said. "Moving on."

"Wait," Paula said, "I'm not finished."

"Then by all means please continue, Miss Outward Bound," Stever said, because Paula had been teaching rock climbing since the age of sixteen. Her legs were the size of boulders.

Paula remembered the morning we set out to go over Thorung La, the pass. Kippy had a bad feeling, and an hour and a half into the trek he made us all turn back. "Just do this for me, okay?" he said. "This is the only thing I'll ever ask of you guys." Everyone grumbled and complained but no one could refuse Kippy when he phrased it like that, like a favor. It turned out there was a blizzard and Kippy most likely saved all of our lives. We waited it out at the base camp for two days before the weather cleared.

I knew there were times Kippy questioned if he was gay, and other times he wouldn't let himself fall asleep because he would wake up in the night gasping for breath, but I didn't think this was relevant so I didn't bring it up. Instead, I told everyone I thought he was genuinely good. When I got sick, he stayed up with me and sang Jon Bon Jovi songs to scare off wild animals while I vomited in the pitch-black woods. He gave me the rest of his Imodium and checked the whites of my eyes. "It would be cool," he told me, "to be a traveling nurse." For three days, he carried my pack along with his and made me drink some kind of electrolyte rehydrating solution. He rested with me every twenty minutes. When I told him I wanted to be a writer, he said, "It's in your destiny. I can feel it in my bones." If I worried about what other people in the group thought of me, or was upset because Paula gave me a dirty look, he'd say, "When you're dead and buried is any of this going to matter?" I told the group I'd trust him with my money, with everything I own, my life. Everyone agreed.

On the last night of the trek, after we'd all eaten and hiked and bled and thrown up together for twenty-six days, someone said, "I'm really going to miss you guys." JC, pissed as he was, started to cry. Kippy said, "Hey, why don't we meet up somewhere?" Someone else said, "Pick a date, any date." Then it was decided. We'd meet again in two months. We were all planning on continuing to travel anyway. We'd each go wherever we were going to go and then meet up in Bangkok. Adam knew a guesthouse that was cheap and clean, and except for the fact that you could hear everything going on in every room and there were grease-spattered signs all over telling you not to throw things out the windows, the place was pretty good.

4.

"It's probably drugs," Jack said at first. "But I don't have much experience with this. JC?"

JC lowered his eyes and picked at a piece of bright blue gum stuck to the sole of his Birkenstock. "I've been on that trip before. It takes a few days."

"Then we should keep an eye on him until it wears off."

We turned to Kippy. He sat on the edge of his cot, arms and legs twisted around himself like a vine. A couple of us walked over and pulled him apart, if only so that he didn't dislocate a shoulder. Paula was ready to take him down if she had to (she worked in a mental ward one summer and knew the best procedure), but there wasn't any need. Kippy didn't try to fight us off; besides, he was easily distracted. He liked to watch the fan on our ceiling. (Who didn't? It looked like it was about to come loose and ricochet around the room.) He'd rest his eyes on various objects—a pile of coins, a runny bar of soap in a Ziploc bag, an orange stick of mosquito repellent, Adam's walking stick (a prop for faking limps), then back to the coins—uncovering a deeper meaning only he could comprehend. If you put a couple of things on his cot, you could occupy him for half an hour. He'd reach out, then withdraw his hand, the way you'd feel for heat over a stove.

We walked down the streets of Bangkok, through alleyways, hustling Kippy around in the middle of us, like a herd of animals guiding and protecting its young. Kippy bounced off one of us or the other. If he became tired, we took him to an outdoor backpacker café where you could order muesli and chopped fruit, and where assertive sparrows took jabs at your toast. A boy there always said, "Orange juice finished," because they never, ever had any, no matter what the menu said. "How about a round of orange juice for the whole restaurant on me?" Stever liked to say first thing to the boy once we figured this out.

Kippy was calm and obedient for the most part, a good sport according to Jack. If we fed him, he chewed thoroughly and swallowed. He didn't dribble juice down the front of his shirt the way they do in the movies. When we put him to sleep at night, laying him on his side, he didn't try to leave the room.

He was quiet, except for every once in a while when he seemed to be deep in conversation with someone who wasn't there. He talked about money a lot, and squabbled over something of his someone was trying to steal. It was as though he were rehearsing lines that needed to be whispered in an overly dramatic way.

5.

On his second morning in Bangkok, in the hall outside of our room, Kippy stuck his hand down his pants and pulled it out smeared with shit.

"Kippy, no!" Stever said, as though talking to a dog, then realizing it, leaned his head back against the wall and said, "Jesus Christ."

The four guys showered Kippy down the hall and swabbed him in deodorant. Paula took his clothes down the street to be washed. I brushed his teeth, staring at the pit where his tooth had once been. "Nothing a dentist can't fix," I said, trying to be cheerful. Kippy looked up at the ceiling while I attempted to floss. When I was done, he stood with his mouth open, lips puckered as though preparing to blow a smoke ring, until I told him it was okay to close it.

When it didn't wear off, we hypothesized. Maybe he'd been drugged and robbed. We'd heard about this happening to a French woman on a bus from Chiang Mai. Or maybe he'd been raped. We'd heard a story about this too, the bottom line being it could happen to guys. Maybe he was on some kind of medication, but it had run out. Maybe he was always this way, but he'd done a good job of hiding it.

"He wasn't always this way," I said. "I know that for a fact."

I didn't, but it sounded good.

"Has anyone looked through his stuff yet?" Jack said. "We could try to find some clues."

Back at the room, we opened Kippy's tent bag, and Jack talked out loud to him, explaining everything we were doing, the way a doctor might when sticking a tongue depressor down your throat.

"We are looking to see what's in your bag, Kippy," Jack said. "We're not exactly sure what happened to you."

Kippy froze at the sound of his name.

Jack loosened the string on the tent bag and dumped everything onto his cot. There was a datebook, a passport, a beach towel, a bag of peanuts, and a pack of playing cards. There were no clothes. Stever peered inside the bag as if expecting to find a severed hand. Jack turned it upside down and sand came pouring out.

"Looks like he was at the beach," Jack said. "Kippy, were you at the beach?"

Kippy flared his nostrils. "Hello, beach!" he said. He pulled a piece of skin off his lip and his lip began to bleed.

"Were you by yourself?" I said.

"The beach is nice," Kippy said. "Very nice."

"Was that a beach in Thailand?" Paula asked.

Kippy stood with his legs three feet apart. "The sand is like salt and pepper."

Jack picked up Kippy's passport and smelled it. He flipped open to the page with Kippy's picture, verifying it was him all along. We already knew his real name was Kenneth, so that came as no surprise. Kippy thought the name was too serious; he said he wouldn't answer to it until he turned thirty.

"I think we can agree he's had some kind of mental breakdown," Jack said. He flipped through Kippy's datebook. Most of the pages were ripped out except for one with an address that said: *IF FOUND, PLEASE SEND TO*…On the inside of the front cover, there was our meeting time and place. *HAPPY LIFE GUESTHOUSE IN BANGKOK! BE THERE OR BE SQUARE!*

"Just like Kippy," Jack said. Then he traced the letters with his finger and said, "Someone must have seen this and brought him here. Otherwise there's no way."

6.

We decided to contact his parents.

"You're the writer in the group," they said. "You do it."

"The writer?" I said.

Paula picked up my notebook and said, "Okay, then what's this?"

I tried to explain there's a difference between wanting to be a writer, and being one. I'd had one article published in *Birdtalk* on how to detect mites but I didn't think that counted. I didn't know fuck-all about birds. I was an administrative assistant until I quit my job to travel.

"Listen," Paula said, picking up my notebook again, "you're the only one who's voluntarily writing a thesis here."

Everyone thought she had a point.

So we got together and wrote a draft, and I was the one with pen in hand. We began, *We are writing to you concerning Kippy's return.* We added, *Kippy has taken ill and we think it would be best if you would come here to Bangkok to pick him up.* Then we said, *Or, if that's not possible, you could wire money and we'll put him on a plane. In that case, you would need to meet him at the other end.* We left the address of the general post office and every piece of information we could think of. We gave directions to the Happy Life Guesthouse where we were staying, but said we didn't think receiving mail there would be very reliable as the travelers' bulletin board downstairs was covered with complaints. At the bottom of the letter, as an afterthought, we wrote, *It would be a relief for all of us to see Kippy in good hands.* I copied down the address from Kippy's datebook. We took the river bus to the post office and sent it off express.

7.

We were continually stopped on the street: tickets to Ko Samui? Night bus to Chiang Mai? Minibus to airport? We shook our heads in unison: nope. People in doorways held up postcards of white-sand beaches and looked at us incredulously: "Why do you stay?"

"Because we're waiting for…" I said, then stopped at the desperation in my voice.

"Where are you going?" a soft-spoken man in a sleeveless denim jacket asked us after we'd said no to him all day. He had dark, bristly eyelashes and blinked in twos and threes.

"We're looking for a ticket to Nowhere," Stever said, voice and eyes lowered, coyly lighting a cigarette, because the man was beautiful. Stever wasn't so shabby himself: in Japan, teenagers had followed him wherever he went. They thought he was Brad Pitt. He claimed to have signed over a thousand autographs.

"Nowhere?" The man raised his hands, exasperated. The nail of his pinkie was long and jagged, uncut.

"You got it," Stever said, scratching his chest. I could have sworn I saw him wink.

8.

From where we were in Bangkok, you could hear round after round of horns blaring in the distance. If you went outside for more than two minutes, you could feel the pollution cling to your skin, creep underneath your fingernails and coat the rims of your eyes. If you blew your nose, something resembling soot came out. You could run a finger across your cheek the way you would a dusty table: it would come up glistening with oil and dirt.

There were vans, buses, planes, and trains coming and going every day, signs in every window in nine different languages saying so. Plans were being made under our noses. Everywhere we went, we stood in someone's way as they left or arrived. People slammed doors and shouted back and forth in French, German, and Hebrew. They pulled up in taxis and noisy tuk-tuks spewing fumes down our throats. Bags were hoisted up and over us, carried across, thrown about. There was an unbelievable amount of people being packed in and out, buses filled to the rim with sweaty limbs dangling out windows to catch whatever feeble breeze there might be.

Our consolation was the pineapple on thin wooden sticks. The man kept them upside down in a large glass jar filled with water. He pulled them out carefully, his bad eye nodding off, and handed them to us one by one. We ate them as you would a melting Popsicle, holding them sideways over the street so that none of the juices dripped down our chins. All the while, the sun beat down on us hard. After, there was a burn to the tongue.

9.

We went to the post office by river bus and watched Styrofoam float by like snowdrifts in our wake. Nothing. We played poker and more poker. We saw a reclining Buddha, a golden Buddha, and one with vapid eyes. We took Kippy to a noodle joint where they welcomed him with open arms because they thought he'd been blessed. We traded our old books in the bookshops on Sukhumvit Road, then traded again for comics. We watched a man milk a snake of its venom. JC cried when we wouldn't let him buy it for a pet. We ate pineapple until our tongues developed thin cuts and bled.

We assessed and condensed our packs, discarding things (a padlock missing a key, corroded batteries) we no longer needed. We changed money, using Scotch tape to piece together any torn—and therefore unacceptable—bills, and counted how many traveler's checks remained. Jack filled up a page of his pocket register with three month's worth of financial transactions, making calculations by picturing an abacus in his head. Adam, tired of strapping a money belt around his waist, searched the room for an ingenious hiding place. Stever walked me down the hall to the sinks, to a handwritten sign that said, *DO NOT THRUST GOODIES OUT WINDOW.* He picked me up, read the sign out loud, pretended to think better of it, put me down.

Adam went out and got his hair cut in the shape of a pineapple, with a little hair-sprayed sprig sticking up on top. Stever helped him wet it and flatten it down. Paula used my razor to shave her armpits, then sniffed them every ten minutes to make sure there was no lingering BO. Stever flipped his mattress, found crusted phlegm on the other side, and flipped it back. JC put moleskin on his heel where the same gobstopper-sized blister kept popping up as if, JC said, to say hello and check in. I borrowed Jack's tweezers to pluck a splinter from Kippy's palm. Jack dropped to the floor in the center of our room and did twenty push-ups, marine-style, sweat dripping down the cleft of his chin and making a small puddle beneath him, while the rest of us fanned ourselves with folded-up pages of the *Bangkok Post* and looked on.

10.

We went back to the post office. Nothing. We returned by the same boat, but stayed on past our stop, until Kippy's tongue crept out of his mouth and draped there like a wilted leaf. At night, we listened to people stagger down the hall past our room into the wee hours, coughing and singing. I heard the guy in the next room flossing his teeth, the ping sound of the string flicking off each tooth. Every so often he'd stop and whisper *fucking fuck fucked up fuck*, as though practicing his conjugations. I imagined him pale, sweating feverishly in the heat, but then again everyone in our guesthouse was pale and sweating feverishly. Stever liked to take off his shirt and wring it out over the sink. Jack, shuffling the cards, said he was sure we would hear something the next day, because even if Kippy had lousy parents, that's what any civilized human being would do. Kippy's hand crept out to his bag of peanuts, fished one out, then darted back into his lap, as though it weren't attached to him, like it was a small, timid animal scurrying for cover.

After a week, we grew too tired to play poker. We played war. The cards were warped by humidity and perspiration. We drank in the mornings and tried to stay buzzed all day. We shelled out baht, and cashed a little more. Our money belts became noticeably lighter. The flies cleaned their wings while we picked our lips. JC tried to feed them crumbs. We pushed away our chairs and strew ourselves like rubble across the lobby floor.

Finally, finally two weeks later there was a letter waiting for us at poste restante. We paid the baht and ripped it open right there. It was three sentences long, on a torn-off page from a legal pad, written in heavy, pooling ink. It said, *WHAT KENNETH NEEDS IS TO STOP HIS SHENANIGANS AND GET BACK TO WORK. I'VE SPOKEN TO HIS BOSS AT THE FACTORY. HIS OLD JOB IS WAITING.*

11.

We walked all the way from the post office to our dorm room, and Stever banged his fist against the wall, making a dent in the plaster.

"I have a fiancée in Denver I need to get back to," he said. This was the first we'd heard about this.

Jack seated Kippy down on his cot and said, "I've got to get myself a summer job to make money for school."

Paula was feeling restless: it was time for her to move on. Adam missed his parents. I was running out of money. JC said he hadn't decided what his next step would be, and he could stay in Bangkok with Kippy and just hang out.

Paula said, "I love you JC, but you really need to get to rehab, get yourself some help." The rest of us looked at the floor and nodded.

I watched Adam screw the top off a water bottle and hand it to Kippy. Kippy sealed his lips around the rim of the bottle and drank. Adam took the bottle away before Kippy could swig the whole thing down, saying, "That's enough now, Kippy. I'll give you more later. You don't want to get a tummy ache now."

"I kind of feel like Kippy's our responsibility," I said, and Stever flipped out.

"We don't even know Kippy," he said, each word encapsulated in a pouch of cigarette smoke. He started pacing, not a good sign.

Paula took a pack of cards out of her pocket and tossed it on Jack's cot. Half the deck spilled over onto the floor. She gave me back the razor I'd lent her, her gaze no higher than my knees.

"Come to think of it," she said, backing away, "you're all strangers."

She lifted up Adam's mattress, where Adam kept his money belt stuffed inside a striped wool sock, and said, "By the way, Adam, this has got to be the worst hiding place in the world. You're so naive. Everyone checks under the mattress. The whole goddamn guesthouse probably knows."

Adam collected his money belt and fastened it around his waist. "I thought it would be good because it was so bad," he said, bowing his head in shame and rocking back on his heels.

"I know you guys," I said. "I do."

"Sure." Paula laughed.

Stever walked around the room seizing what he claimed was rightfully his and lobbing it into a heap on his cot. It appeared he thought everything belonged to him. There was a mad dash of the rest of us rifling through his pile, weeding out what was ours, clothes flying across the room, a pair of tighty-whities snared by the ceiling fan, a shouting match over a crushed pack of Longlife cigarettes. A mist of down sprayed out from Paula's sleeping bag, and Adam's walking stick snapped in half. We each hoarded our own stuff in hills around the room and stood guard to ward off plunderers. Except for Jack, who sat with ankle over knee and observed us as though we were bizarre, hyperactive rodents in a lab.

"All right, all right," Jack said, flicking the lights off and on. "Have we gotten it out of our systems?"

12.

We agreed to keep calm and call a meeting downstairs. We walked down the cement steps in double file. We sat around our usual white plastic table and ordered a round of shots, shelling out three or four times more baht than we normally would. We lit cigarettes with Paula's Zippo. JC grabbed a plate of uneaten curry rice from the next table over and took a bite using the fork that came with it. None of us had the energy to register our disgust.

We looked at Kippy. He'd developed creases sprouting across his forehead and forking out the corners of his eyes, the etchings of a person lost in thought. He had a sparse beard—whiskers, really—that, like a cobweb, you could see only in reflected light. His lips were preparing to molt.

We discussed scenarios. We examined options. Jack unfolded a blank piece of paper he kept in his pocket, fuzzy from going through the wash. He listed pros and cons and made projections that spiraled around the border of the page and ended where they began. We talked about pooling money together and one of us escorting Kippy back to the States. But what would that person do with him once he got him there?

The fact of the matter was: he could function, he could talk. He wasn't violent or foaming at the mouth. He didn't have open sores oozing puss. He could breathe, chew, cough, and swallow. He'd been like this for God knows how long without us, and he was doing fine. There were others like him too. Every so often, you'd run across a traveler babbling Bible verses and staring at his hands or sleeping on newspaper behind the door of a train station. In traveling, as in life, there were no guarantees.

Paula said, "I hate to say it but he's much better off here than back home." She motioned to Kippy's parents' letter, which was curled up in the middle of the table like a scroll, and was already going soft from us opening it and smoothing it out and rolling it closed again.

Jack nodded. "He always wanted to travel."

Adam pressed a tooth that had been bothering him and grimaced. "This is his dream."

Stever suggested we pay for Kippy to stay on at the guesthouse, but Jack said once he went out, he probably wouldn't be able to find his way back to the room. He wouldn't be tracking time. We'd have to accept that he'd be roaming free.

"Without a home base?" I said.

"I haven't had one since I was thirteen," Paula scoffed, dashing her cigarette against the heel of her sandal.

Adam brought up the point that people in Thailand always gave food to the poor. There were even bowls of rice set out for the stray dogs. "No one starves here," he said.

JC agreed, patting his stomach.

"You mean we're going to ditch him?" I said. "Just like that?"

"Don't you see?" Stever said, pressing his fingertips white against his skull, as if he were pasting something there, waiting for the glue to dry. "We're saving him from the assembly line."

"More like an institution," Paula said.

"Paula's right," Jack said. "If he goes back, there's the chance he'll be locked up."

JC eyed an abandoned bag of Fritos across the room. "What if they throw away the key?"

They scooted their chairs in towards me, surrounding me, probably thinking I might get up and run. I couldn't look at them. I picked at a scab on my shin until Jack bent down and put a hand over it to stop me.

"I know this is what he would want," Adam said.

I did a shot of something swirly and brown that tasted like turpentine and wiped my mouth on my forearm. Stever nodded at me with approval.

"Why don't we ask Kippy himself?" I said.

Kippy sat at the end of the table, shredding a napkin and licking the pieces as if they were stamps.

"Do you want to stay here or go home?" Jack said.

"I've always liked you," Kippy said.

"Could you live here by yourself?" I said.

Kippy picked the napkin off his tongue. "I should say so."

13.

This is the hard part to explain, the part I don't think I'd understand if I hadn't been there myself. It seemed right at the time, although now I've become less and less sure. We packed Kippy's green tent bag with food, water, and small denominations of bills. Paula made him put on a pair of drawstring cotton pants she bought for him at the weekend market. Jack smeared Kippy's face and arms with sunblock. Adam dabbed calamine lotion on an infected bug bite above his eyelid. I took off my turquoise necklace and put it around Kippy's neck, then kissed him on the lips. Stever, one-upping me, hugged Kippy and picked him up and rocked him in his arms.

We ordered him a large plate of phat thai with an extra heaping of bean sprouts. We watched him eat, and got excited when he inhaled more noodles at once than could possibly fit in his mouth. We gave him two glasses of water to wash down the food and patted him on the back in case he needed to burp. For the last time, I led him to the nearest faucet and brushed his teeth, but I didn't have to say anything, because by then he knew when to open his mouth and when to close it.

We took him to Khoa San Road, lined with travel agencies, cafés, and sidewalk stalls, where backpackers with wild, overrun hair flocked up and down in colorful, mismatched clothes. Travelers called to one another across stalled traffic ("Hey you, didn't we sleep together in Goa last year?"), haggled with shopkeepers over batiks that smelled of incense, and laughed too loudly at unspoken jokes. We didn't think the commotion would bother Kippy, but we did a couple of laps on both sides of the street, passing hawkers and vendors displaying their wares, to be sure. Even when a cassette seller blasted his boom box in our faces, Kippy didn't mind.

Then we stopped in the middle of everything, spun him around, and set him free.

The first thing that happened was some asshole in imitation military fatigues walked straight into him and knocked him over. Kippy fell flat on his back and didn't move. I wanted to help, but Stever held me back, massaging my shoulders, saying, "Rachel, let's just wait and see."

Kippy lay on the sidewalk, legs splayed out, arms stiff at his sides. A Japanese tour group nearly tripped over him, until the leader blew a whistle and instructed everyone to lower their cameras away from their faces and tiptoe around him, using quiet, exaggerated steps. A couple of school children in white blouses and black shorts poked Kippy with a stick and dodged behind a cart selling grilled bananas. A sparrow flew down and pecked Kippy's ear. I moved, but Stever caught me.

Kippy rolled onto his side and pushed himself up into a half-lotus position. A young woman with a Canadian flag sewn onto her pack gave him a hand and pulled him up, and in one of the kindest gestures I've seen in my life, brushed him off.

We were so happy we cheered.

14.

I was the last to leave Bangkok, maybe because I was the only one who didn't have anything too thrilling to bring me back. I was going to have to find a place to live and a job, not my two favorite things to do. I'd been traveling for over two years.

Kippy told me things I needed to hear. He said, "You and I are too sensitive for this world. We need to brace ourselves. It's a wonder we survive." We were platonic, always were. (Who wants to compete with Paula? Not me.) Except for one drunken kiss in the countryside of Nepal, in a teahouse that no longer exists. Most of what we experienced has been built over, torn down.

Those days in Bangkok, before we knew what we were going to do, I tried talking to him, pulling him aside, saying, "It's me, Rachel. I'm here," and "Why don't we pick up where we left off?" Once, I put my arms around him, but it felt like I was hugging a bale of straw. For a while, I tried to convince myself I made a difference. In the end, I'm not sure if it amounted to anything at all, if he could hear or understand me.

If I were to run into Kippy now, say in an elevator somewhere, in my usual business attire, my hair bobbed, would he know me? If I asked him to press the fourth floor for me would he recognize the sound of my voice?

A week after we let Kippy go, I went back to Khoa San Road and searched for him. I told myself if Kippy looked like he needed help then I would take him with me and figure something out. If he was okay, I would leave without letting him know I was there. I found him sitting on the stoop of a batik shop, only a couple of blocks away from where we'd left him. He had a tie-dyed sarong looped around his shoulders like a cape, and seemed to have befriended a bearded traveler in a ski hat. They were picking through a pile of things they appeared to have hoarded. I crept closer to get a better look. I glimpsed the buckle of a belt, a half-eaten bun, a thimble, a child's shoe. "So many beginnings and endings," I heard Kippy say. "Man, oh man, oh man," his friend said, lifting his shirt to dab the sweat on his forehead.

15.

I get letters from those guys. I still do. Most of them are back home married with kids, except for Paula who teaches outdoor leadership courses in Kenya. I became a commercial liability underwriter for an insurance agency. Stever broke up with his longtime fiancée and ended up marrying someone he'd known for three weeks. (Isn't that the way it always works out?) JC went into rehab and came out clean. NA is his religion. Adam works in real estate. Jack teaches at a university in London. None of us are rich or famous. We exchange cards every year around the holidays, and I've come to dread it, down to the core, the very bone. There is something about the propped-up babies, the plastered smiles, the tinselly decorations that remind me of fish trapped in a frozen pond.

Can a traveler ever blend back into life? Can you ever fully return from where you've once been? I can't settle down (most of my stuff is in boxes and my walls are bare), yet in the past eight years I haven't gone anywhere. I don't own a bike or a car. During the day, I sit in my office with my back to a window that looks down onto a parking lot with a pay booth. I rub my stockinged feet against the new speckled carpet to keep warm. I type, and when people stand in my doorway I hold up a finger to let them know I am in the middle of a sentence but will be with them momentarily. At night, I dream that Kippy is drinking rain, mouth open to the sky, and I'll eventually find him. I push my way through crowded street markets and train stations shouting, Has anyone heard from Kippy? Is he all right?

WILLOW
SPRINGS
BOOKS

Willow Springs Books is a small literary press housed in Eastern Washington University's Inland Northwest Center for Writers, in Spokane. The staff of Willow Springs Books is comprised of creative writing graduate and undergraduate students. As part of an internship for which they receive college credit, the students get hands-on experience in every phase of the publishing process. Willow Springs Books' staff oversees the annual Spokane Prize for Short Fiction competition. They also publish annually one surrealist poetry chapbook.

Willow Springs Books staff who contributed to this book include Derek Annis, Katie Bell, Jess L. Bryant, Russ Deniston, Vladislav Frederick, Austin Fuller, Lauren Hohle, Paulina Garcia, Robin Golke, Andrew Koch, Hannah Koeske, Daniel Matthewson, Jared Reed, Megan Rowe, Michael Schmidt, Charlene Shepard, Clarinda Simpson, Anthony Stillinger, Kyle Thiele, Nicholas Thomas, and Lexi Watkins.

LOST HORSE PRESS

THE SPOKANE PRIZE FOR SHORT FICTION

The Spokane Prize for Short Fiction is made possible through the partnership of Lost Horse Press and Willow Springs Books. Based in Sandpoint, Idaho, Lost Horse Press is a 501(c)(3) nonprofit, independent press that publishes the works of established as well as emerging poets, and makes available fine contemporary literature through cultural, educational and publishing programs and activities. This and other Lost Horse Press titles may be viewed online at losthorsepress.org. Previous winners of the Spokane Prize for Short Fiction as well as Willow Springs Books chapbooks can be viewed at willowspringsbooks.org.